"I was challenged by this book to think freshly about Jesus. *Amazed: Why the Humanity of Jesus Matters* serves as a guide to consider anew our understanding of and life with Jesus, not only as God but also as man. As the book unfolds, we discover the gift of our humanity and how that shapes how we are supposed to be with each other and with God. If I did not recognize this before, I now understand that Richard Bahr is a uniquely qualified guide on our journey to knowing Jesus. Richard has truly given us a gift in this exceptional book. It is ideal for all who have a deep sense that there is more to Jesus than we have thought, dreamed, or imagined."

Captain Katherine Clausell
Administrator, The Salvation Army Harbor Light Center

"*Amazed: Why the Humanity of Jesus Matters* forces us to wrestle with the humanity that Jesus had more than two thousand years ago. The book challenges us to see Jesus through the lens of the time that he spent walking on this earth. Richard Bahr uses the truth and authority of Scripture to give us the opportunity to see Jesus in a new light. I loved the conviction and honesty Richard uses to show the way Jesus handled the same everyday situations that we encounter in life. This book will encourage you. Deeply. It will call you to see the human side of the man who changed the world and give you the chance to experience him on a new level."

Josh Christenson
Lead Pastor, Imagine Church

"It is often hard to identify with Jesus—a life without sin, complete obedience to the Father, and miracles by command. In his book *Amazed: Why the Humanity of Jesus Matters*, Richard Bahr helped me relate to Jesus. By helping me focus not just on Jesus' divine nature but drawing my attention to his humanity, this book allowed me to identify in new ways the image of God working inside of me. If you desire to model your life after Jesus, this study on his humanity is a great place to begin building your foundation."

Nate Kemper
Lead Pastor, Nowthen Alliance Church

amazed

amazed

WHY THE
HUMANITY OF JESUS
MATTERS

by Richard Bahr

HPA | HUFF PUBLISHING ASSOCIATES

MINNEAPOLIS

THRESHOLD
to New Life™ •

Acts 4:32-33

www.threshold2newlife.org

To my Dad and Mom

They were the first version of the humanity of Jesus I experienced.

"Have you ever commanded the morning to appear and caused the dawn to rise in the east?" Job 38:12

Contents

INTRODUCTION

I set out a couple of years ago to get to know Jesus better. I picked up a suggestion to read and then reread the gospels in the Bible, the first four books of the New Testament: Matthew, Mark, Luke, and John. These four books are eyewitness accounts of Jesus' life and contain the words he spoke. They were written to document his lifetime on earth.

I read the gospels over and over for some period of time. I don't recall how long it was suggested to keep reading these books. I'm at about twenty months as of this writing. I'm still reading them.

Many things struck me about this man Jesus. He was kind, gentle, bold, patient, wise, and humble just to name a few of his character traits. This is the kind of guy I would like to hang around. This is the kind of guy I would like to be.

HE BECAME HUMAN

It is significant that Jesus *became* a man. In his gospel, the apostle John indicates that Jesus has two distinct natures—both man and God. I have thought a lot about Jesus being God but have never really thought about him also being a man. The first time I had a real encounter with this reality was while reading the account in Luke of Jesus and the Roman centurion (covered in chapter 6). Jesus was "amazed" at the centurion's faith, which was the inspiration for the title of this book. I was amazed that Jesus could be amazed. And there are many other examples in the gospels of Jesus in his humanity, which I guess I knew, but rarely ever thought about it. Jesus was actually a physical, living, breathing man.

UNEXPECTED KINGDOM

Fundamental to the belief of anyone identifying himself or herself as Christian is that Jesus Christ is the long-awaited-for and much-prophesied-about Messiah. Much of the biblical Old Testament points to his arrival. The Messiah was promised and expected to deliver the Jewish people from centuries of oppression.

In his time on earth in human flesh, Jesus talked about a kingdom that was misunderstood by others. Most of his followers and even his closest associates (the disciples) expected him to overthrow the Roman government, take back Jerusalem, and become their earthly ruler.

With the benefit of hindsight, we can see by our reading of the gospels this wasn't his intent at all. There was no precedent for a king to come as Jesus did. No one imagined that God would come to earth as a man to live, eat, walk, talk, and generally hang out with a bunch of people for about thirty-three years. It wasn't what anyone expected. God delivered his kingdom through Jesus, and as usual, his plan was perfect as well as a surprise on a cosmic level.

Not until Jesus' physical death, the discovery of the empty tomb, his disciples seeing and touching his resurrected body, and finally his ascension from their physical presence did Jesus' plan and kingdom begin to sink in with the disciples.

Finally they got it. Got it in a big way.

Eventually the apostle Peter became the "rock" of the church. He became a dynamic preacher and a fearless leader. But shortly before Jesus' crucifixion, the same Peter denied even knowing Jesus upon being confronted. Peter and the others finally understood that Jesus' kingdom would come through our living with the Holy Spirit he left for us, and we're promised to come into the fullness of his kingdom after his second coming. In Peter, the mouse became the minister. Jesus has that kind of impact on us when we allow it.

TROUBLE SEEING TWO NATURES

In his time on earth while Jesus was living as a man, did the disciples and his followers have difficulty seeing Jesus as a real person?

I don't think so. I think it was rather easy for them to see Jesus as a man. He was as much a real person as any of them were. They touched him. He had physical needs as they did. He ate meals. He slept. No problem to see Jesus as a man.

Let's face it; it's a significant leap to think of and see a man as God. To see Jesus as God seemed to be a bit of a transformation process that took time to sink in. But for the disciples to see Jesus as a *man?* Not too tough.

How about for us? We don't currently have the benefit of actually walking, talking, and eating with Jesus in a physical realm. The disciples and the earlier followers had the benefit of spending time with Jesus in his humanity—hanging out, eating, being taught by him, fishing, walking from place to place, all the normal activities of the day. We're left only with the eyewitness accounts of others that we're challenged to believe.

Here we are roughly two thousand years later. Belief in and worship of Jesus continues to this day. We worship Jesus. We pray to Jesus.

We wear tattoos and jewelry symbolizing his sacrifice on the cross. We sing songs about Jesus. We read books written in our present day about him. We put bumper stickers on our cars. Jesus is God. To me there seems to be no doubt about that.

And we spend a lot of time on that subject. Jesus is God; he is our savior and redeemer. It is the central message of all Christian churches—Jesus' coming as a baby in the manger in Bethlehem to his sacrifice on the cross at Easter. Jesus is God.

In the time before Jesus, people mostly approached God through designates. The priests, Levites, and sometimes prophets seemed to have a direct connection to communicate with God—listening, delivering his messages, and petitioning him with requests and concerns. Jesus changed all that. In John 14:6 Jesus describes himself as the only way to the father. Wow. The phone system was rewired; the protocol changed. Now, Jesus is the hot line to God. We need no other.

So the people who lived with the man Jesus had trouble seeing him as God. For all of their lives and the lives of their parents, grandparents, and so on for dozens of generations back, people accessed God through others. And there were lots of rules about everything from what to eat, how to wash, and how to worship. This was what the disciples and early followers of Jesus knew. It was their paradigm. You can imagine this was no small thing to have these folks begin to see the world differently.

We who have not lived with the man Jesus see him as God and may not think often of him as a man. Much of our emphasis in worship, study, and prayer is contemplating that Jesus is God. As it should be. But could it be important to see Jesus as a man as well as God?

ADDICTS' PERFECT SPONSOR

When drug addicts or alcoholics are early in their stages of recovery, who is best for them to talk to, ask questions of, and pattern their life after? Do they seek this from their local auto mechanic? How about their dentist? A high school teacher?

Those in early recovery from chemical dependency are urged to meet and get to know someone they can relate to who has been in their shoes. Someone who has struggled as they have struggled, dealt with the compulsions, been saddled with the legal problems and interpersonal relationship pain, and felt the urges that only one who has suffered with addiction has felt. Addicts in successful long-term recovery know the challenges. They can empathize with the struggles. They know the pain and the temptations. And they have persevered. Long-term recovering addicts can sponsor and show newcomers the path to freedom from drugs and alcohol. They know the way because they've lived it. And they can provide hope. "Follow me," says the sponsor, for a better way of life.

"Follow me," Jesus said over and over as recorded in the New Testament. If it were recorded once, it would be important and true. Five or six times we should probably sit up and take notice. It's recorded more than a dozen times. Hmmm . . . there must be something to that.

We are all addicts. Addicted to sin. We were born into this condition that has no cure this side of heaven. It can only be treated. The flavors of choice of our sins are many: chemicals, sex, materialism, self-sufficiency, overeating, laziness, overworking, gossiping, egoism, and the list goes on. If it stands between God and the fullness of life he has for us, he wants it eliminated. We can't do it alone. But there is a way.

THE PERFECT LIFE

I like the idea that the king of all kings, the maker and ruler of the whole universe, the one in control of all things came to live as I live. He felt what I feel. He was tempted as I am tempted. He had physical needs as I do. He felt sorrow. He became angry. He submitted. I like to think of him in the midst of all these trials in his humanity—persevering, never wavering, always getting it right. He drew his strength from his Father. Now he gives me the same access. The same power. The power available from the Holy Spirit.

Jesus lived a perfect life. He did it while in the flesh, as a man, not because he needed to, but because *we* need him to. He is the perfect sponsor, as the long-term sober addict is to the addict new to recovery. I realize it seems not to be the perfect comparison but go with me on this for a moment. He struggled and suffered. I struggle and suffer. He did it perfectly, relying on his Father. He's the best example for me to follow. Might that be why it's recorded that Jesus said "follow me" so often in the gospels? Of course, Jesus is more than simply our "sponsor"; however, I do like the idea of him being a man and walking the same paths in life I have walked, and that he can relate to me and I to him.

PERSONAL RELATIONSHIP

I don't recall the first time I was asked; I was probably a teenager. Someone queried me if I had a personal relationship with Jesus. Personal? That puzzled me for a long time. A personal relationship with Jesus? With God? Why not a personal relationship with God? Can we do that?

My hope for you in reading this book is that you'll develop a deeper, personal connection to Jesus by really understanding there was a critical purpose for him to come to earth as a person like you and me. This wasn't a random act or a nice little thing to do. It just may be God's perfect plan to restore us into the relationship with him he wants for us. God's perfect plan. To come in a way to which we can relate. To live as we live. To struggle and suffer like us.

We are hardwired to connect with other people. We are made to be relational. We get married. We have friends. We get lonely. All because God made us in such a way that we need others. He knows that. It's his design. So Jesus came as a man—as one of us. What better way to connect with us than by being one of us?

A personal relationship with Jesus is available to us. In my case, understanding better the fact that he was a man and lived a life on earth as I do, helps me relate better. It helps my faith become a little more personal. I'm beginning to understand a little better how I can develop a personal relationship with Jesus. I hope you will too.

amazed

JESUS
WAS PHYSICAL

The next morning as they were leaving Bethany, Jesus was hungry.

Mark 11:12

Jesus became God incarnate, coming to earth in human form when he was born to a virgin woman named Mary more than two thousand years ago. He was an actual, physical being and experienced a physical life just as you and I.

Being physical can be really great! There might have been a time in your life that you were able (and maybe liked) to run, jump, and play a sport that required you to be physical. Maybe you still do. Have you ever received a back rub or a massage? Mmmm . . . that is very relaxing and physical. To smell a flower, see a sunset, or hug your children, grandchildren, and many others are all enjoyable physical acts. God makes us physical, and being physical can be such a blessing.

So how about the downside? Sickness, sleeplessness, physical pain, migraines, loss of sight, and struggles to make it up the stairs as we age. And how about cancer? That is a terrible thing in our physical realm.

The human race brought that on. Originally none of the previously mentioned negative stuff existed. But when we stopped trusting God, decided we knew better, and could run our lives just fine on our own, well, that's when it happened.

> Then he said to the woman, "I will sharpen the pain of your pregnancy, and in pain you will give birth." **Genesis 3:16a**

> And to the man he said, "Since you listened to your wife and ate from the tree whose fruit I commanded you not to eat, the ground is cursed because of you. All your life you will struggle to scratch a living from it." **Genesis 3:17**

So we're in for a life of physical challenges, such as painful childbirth and hard work. Ultimately our life on earth ends with a physical death. And in a life apart from God, there would be no more for us. But that's why Jesus came to restore our relationship with God and ultimately his creation back to the way God designed and desires it. Since it can be tough to live here on earth as a person, I wonder if that's why God came to us as a person. So we could better connect with him since we know he has lived just as we live? And Jesus struggled at times just as we struggle now.

The birth and youth of Jesus

There is not much recorded in the Bible about Jesus' life before his earthly ministry began when he was about thirty years old. The most detailed account of Jesus' birth is recorded in the gospel of Luke. When the Christmas story is read aloud, this is often the account used. Luke, the author, was a physician. As fitting his profession, his account is detailed, and the writing is very precise. I have wondered whether anyone was able to read his handwriting! Okay, perhaps a poorly placed joke. (But, now that I've pointed that out, I bet you're curious too.)

Many people have heard this story. Young mother, traveled far, holed up in a stable, gave birth, laid the baby in a manger (an animal feeding trough), and then entertained guests that stopped to visit and give gifts.

It is widely thought that Mary was probably a teenager. Imagine that! An angel told her that she would be pregnant with a baby—without human intervention. How would she explain that to her fiancé? With more than two thousand years of hindsight there is more acceptance of this. However, Mary and Joseph were real people. Think how difficult that situation would have been to explain. And in the culture of the time, a woman pregnant out of wedlock was not as accepted as she would be today. Joseph had tremendous courage to marry her. I wonder if he put up with a lot of grief from his friends and family.

Luke mentions that the baby was circumcised, as was customary for a child born to Jewish parents, and he was given the name Jesus. Little is written about Jesus as a youth. He was raised in the town of Nazareth, grew up healthy and strong, and was a bright and mature young man. Without Luke's commentary, we'd know even less than we do about Jesus as a child and youth.

There the child grew up healthy and strong. He was filled with wisdom, and God's favor was on him. Luke 2:40

Think for a moment what it would be like to raise Jesus or be his sister or brother. He was a real kid, just like we all have been. In that time as the oldest son, he might have spent a lot of time with his father and might have been trained in his dad's trade to follow in his footsteps. He might also have had duties around the house, feeding their animals or looking after the younger children while his parents ran an errand.

What would it have been like being a brother or sister to Jesus and growing up with him? He might have played games with the other kids and done all the things any other child of the period and region would have done. I was the kind of kid that seemed often to find trouble. I think I spent most of elementary school sitting in the front of the class so the teacher could keep an eye on me. If Jesus would have been my big brother, I can see myself saying to our mother, "Hey, how come Jesus never gets a time out?" Her answer might be, "Because he hasn't done anything wrong."

It is interesting to think about what a young Jesus might have been like. Scripture leaves us to simply wonder about much of his childhood and upbringing.

MEALTIME

Jesus felt hungry. This is mentioned multiple times in the gospels.

Our physical bodies are designed with the need for both food and water. We ingest food, which our digestive system breaks down to convert to fuel our bodies can burn. Much like an automobile, we need fuel to operate effectively. Food and water are the fuel.

Jesus inhabited a physical body that operated on the very same physical principles that are at work today in our physical bodies. Being human, Jesus needed food to provide for his body. He felt hunger and thirst just as we do.

> *For forty days and forty nights he fasted and became very hungry.*
> Matthew 4:2

> *The next morning as they were leaving Bethany, Jesus was hungry.*
> Mark 11:12

If reading this while a member of a developed nation in today's world, it is unlikely you have felt hunger the way others do in less developed nations. Hunger ravages the body, with the body literally eating itself to survive. Extreme hunger is deadly. So can gluttony—the habit of overeating—be unhealthy for our bodies. In the United States, poor eating habits have been traced to all sorts of disease, like diabetes, which diminish the quality of one's life and can ultimately kill. Anorexia and bulimia are both conditions that cause many people to struggle and are examples of how people of a broken world wrestle with something as basic as how to feed themselves.

It's so interesting that this glorious gift of food can be turned into such a problem by the human race. Think about the smell of fresh caramel rolls baking in the oven. The aroma wafting from an Italian restaurant. What about the process of barbequing steak or ribs? God provided all these experiences—the smell, taste, and visual appearance as well as the companionship when enjoying a great meal—for our pleasure. And the process of consumption also has a useful purpose, which God created to refuel our bodies into something wonderful.

Yet people overeat, have poor eating habits, or struggle with having enough good food to eat. They have anxiety over the unhealthy and untrue images of their bodies produced by eating. And there are many parts of this world that don't have enough food and clean water. There people toil each day to raise only a little food and water to share among their families. How is it that something so good can get so messed up?

Jesus came to change all of this. To provide us relief from our nature to goof up and wrestle with all the good God provided in this world, like a tasty meal. After Jesus fed the five thousand on the shores of the Sea of Galilee, people followed after him the next day, providing Jesus with a teachable moment. When they asked for more of the bread, just as God had provided their ancestors through Moses, Jesus answered their question in a way only he could.

> Jesus replied, "I am the bread of life. Whoever comes to me will never be hungry again." John 6:35a

My wife, Carla, and I work in a local ministry that helps close gaps in peoples' lives when they're moving forward yet hit some sort of a snag or setback. Sometimes we simply provide a referral to an agency that can provide specific assistance but oftentimes we get involved in sourcing furniture, interview clothing, or a variety of other things. The most common request is to provide some financial relief for rent or utilities.

I am frequently humbled and awed at the great faith and perspective of so many of our clients. When we finish the meeting at which we take the client's application, we often ask if there is anything they want us to pray with them about. I've never once had someone request prayer to win the lottery. The requests are modest, basic stuff, and a sincere appreciation for our organization being involved to help out. So many of our clients have come so far in life and have great, inspiring testimonies they share with us of how God has stepped in to help them. Prayerful petitions to God to provide for our basic existence have been a common request since the dawn of humankind.

Jesus provides and sustains us. He provides for all of our needs.

> *"That is why I tell you not to worry about everyday life—whether you have enough food and drink, or enough clothes to wear. Isn't life more than food, and your body more than clothing? Look at the birds. They don't plant or harvest or store food in barns, for your heavenly Father feeds them. And aren't you far more valuable to him than they are?"* Matthew 6:25–26

In 1988 Bobby McFerrin released a song that became a cultural icon titled "Don't Worry, Be Happy." This sounds simple but let's face it, we've all been through situations in our lives that make this seem impossible. I might suggest an alternate version of the title and lyrics that contain a greater truth—"Don't Worry, Follow Him."

NEED SOMETHING TO DRINK

I mentioned water earlier. Water is a common life-giving element that is required by all living things. Unquenched thirst, like long-term hunger, is a terrible plight to experience. Much of the travel done by people in Jesus' time was on foot. Jesus traveled on foot. Journeys could be hundreds of miles, inconceivable for those of us nowadays with multiple means of automated transportation. When is the last time you walked a hundred miles in a dry, dusty, hot environment?

Jesus experienced thirst. During a road trip heading through Samaria, he came to a village that had an ancient, legendary well—Jacob's well. He was tired from the long journey and sat down to rest. A local woman came to the well to draw water, so she likely had the tools with her to do so—a bucket and a rope. Jesus was thirsty, and when he saw that someone had the means to fetch some water out of the well, he began a dialogue with the woman.

> *Soon a Samaritan women came to draw water, and Jesus said to her, "Please give me a drink."* John 4:7

This began a conversation between the woman and Jesus. He turned this talk from a simple request for a drink of water into a life-altering moment by offering her "living water." Not only this but Jesus explained how to get the living water and introduced himself as the Messiah whom she had been waiting upon. She was so excited she ran off to her village, leaving her water-carrying jar behind, to notify the others that the man at the well might be the Messiah.

Another mention of Jesus' thirst is during his crucifixion while hanging and dying on the cross.

> *Jesus knew that his mission was now finished, and to fulfill Scripture he said, "I am thirsty."* John 19:28

Most Bibles highlight references to other related texts. This John verse points to Psalm 22:15 and Psalm 69:21 as evidence that Jesus, while hanging on the cross and near physical death, had the presence of mind to fulfill scripture by asking for something to drink. Not only for this purpose, but one could only figure that in Jesus' condition, suspended above the ground, nailed to a cross, and exposed to the midday Middle Eastern sun that he would have been suffering from significant thirst.

Jesus has an answer to our thirst, just as he does with our hunger.

> "Whoever believes in me will never be thirsty." John 6:35b

> "Anyone who believes in me may come and drink! For the Scriptures declare, 'Rivers of living water will flow from his heart.'"
> John 7:38

This additional reference made by Jesus to "living water" continues on to explain that living water is the Holy Spirit, which is given to all who choose to believe in him. We encounter the Holy Spirit once our lives are surrendered, without holding back, and we continue to experience living water when we worship, drink in his word, and commune with him in prayer.

THE SLEEPY KING

Jesus also became physically tired.

> Jesus was sleeping at the back of the boat with his head on a cushion. Mark 4:38a

> Before daybreak the next morning, Jesus got up and went out to an isolated place to pray. Mark 1:35

We've all felt tired. Long nights awake during finals week in college. Maybe while our child was teething and it was our turn to stay up to be the consoling parent. Perhaps waiting up for the same kid as a teenager when missing a curfew and not answering the phone, worried sick that something bad happened. Or we might have a condition like sleep apnea that inhibits our ability to get good rest. We attempt sleep and think we are sleeping, but wake up in the morning and go throughout the day groggy and dull. Sleep is another part of being physical. People need sleep. We all do. And in his humanness, Jesus slept too.

A pattern is developing. Each of these elements of our physical nature are God-given and part of his creation. In our human nature, we often find ways to mess up and push to unnatural limits all of these good things. Things like eating, drinking, and sleeping can be very good and natural. Once again, Jesus has the ultimate answer for our need to have rest.

> Then Jesus said, "Come to me, all of you who are weary and carry heavy burdens, and I will give you rest. Take my yoke upon you. Let me teach you, because I am humble and gentle at heart, and you will find rest for your souls. For my yoke is easy to bear, and the burden I give you is light." Matthew 11:28-30

Is it a relief to you that Jesus can and will carry your burdens? He said, "I will give you rest." Are you in need of rest? He will provide you that rest. We worry about the future and lament over our struggles and failures of our past. Left alone with this we have no way to find rest. Jesus promises that we will find rest for our souls through him. Whew! When I turn things over to him, I find this to be true. Sure, I don't do this right away. It seems I'd rather struggle for a while. Why is that anyway? Once I'm tired of wrestling with my issues on my own, I come to the cross with my hurts and worries, and Jesus starts me on a new path that provides me the relief that only he can provide.

UNIMAGINABLE PAIN

Another aspect to Jesus' physical nature was his experience during his trial and crucifixion.

When arrested in the garden of Gethsemane, Jesus was betrayed by one of his close followers. The betrayer, Judas, had a prearranged signal with the soldiers to identify the man that was the object of their search. Earlier, Judas had traded his knowledge of Jesus' whereabouts for thirty pieces of silver.

Then Judas Iscariot, one of the twelve disciples, went to the leading priests and asked, "How much will you pay me to betray Jesus to you?" And they gave him thirty pieces of silver. Matthew 26:14–15

Judas walked over to Jesus to greet him with a kiss. Luke 22:47b

So Jesus received a kiss. Not an affectionate one, but a kiss that set in motion the events that were foretold centuries before.

Even my best friend, the one I trusted completely, the one who shared my food, has turned against me. Psalm 41:9

And I said to them, "If you like, give me my wages, whatever I am worth; but only if you want to." So they counted out for my wages thirty pieces of silver. Zechariah 11:12

Once in captivity, Jesus was led from place to place to meet with his accusers. During this time, Jesus was severely beaten with sticks, pummeled by the fists of his captors, and whipped with an inhuman instrument of torture.

And they spit on him and grabbed the stick and struck him on the head with it. Matthew 27:30

Then Pilate had Jesus flogged with a lead-tipped whip. The soldiers wove a crown of thorns and put it on his head, and they put a purple robe on him, "Hail! King of the Jews!" they mocked, as they slapped him across the face. John 19:1–3

The Bible television show and the *Son of God* movie by Mark Burnett and Roma Downey show visual depictions of the physical torment and murder of Jesus on the cross. There are others too. In common are the indescribable atrocity, inhuman treatment, and physical agony and suffering experienced by Jesus. Knowing that this is a depiction of the one to whom I owe my very life, it is extremely painful to watch.

Jesus also endured scourging, the process of whipping or lashing the body with leather straps that contained embedded metal and/or bone fragments designed to tear the flesh from the body. The crown of thorns placed upon his head is thought to be made of a hard wood, such as oak or the like, which is used to make sturdy furniture, with the thorns being one to two inch spikes that would pierce the skin and perhaps even the bone of the skull.

Crucifixion is considered one of the most inhuman and cruel forms of punishment, bringing certain death to those experiencing it. A crucified person was stripped naked and hanged above the ground on a rough-sawn, two-timbered cross. Large nails, possibly three quarters of an inch wide and six to eight inches long were hammered through Jesus' wrists and one through both feet. His knees were slightly bent to provide for the means to push up with his feet to allow for the ability to take a breath. So he hung there, naked, going through the process of pushing up on his nail-pierced feet each time to take a breath, then collapse again on the same bloody, nail-pierced feet, only to do this again each time a breath was needed.

The physical body of Jesus was bruised and bleeding during this torturous process. Emotionally it would have been excruciating to experience the trauma brought on during this abuse. Jesus experienced this. He did it for me and for you too.

Once he was nailed to the cross and raised erect, hanging by the large spikes that pierced his body, hours later he drew his last breath and died a physical death.

> When Jesus had tasted it, he said, "It is finished!" Then he bowed his head and released his spirit.   John 19:30

Jesus' body was removed from the cross and taken by Joseph of Arimathea, a leader of the Jews and a secret follower of Jesus, to be prepared for burial. His body was entombed and sealed with a large rock. The tomb was guarded by Roman soldiers so that no one could steal the body and then claim Jesus was raised from the dead. Both the Roman and Jewish leaders were well aware of Jesus' claims and teachings.

Unless Jesus comes again during our lifetime, we face the same fate. Our physical bodies will fail, and we will pass into physical death. Unpleasant to consider, however true. Jesus experienced this. He did it so we will have life after death and be given new bodies, just as he has.

THE RESURRECTION

Lastly, Jesus was physical after his resurrection.

The primary objective of this book is to examine Jesus in his humanity. So once he died and was resurrected, was he still in his humanity? Scripture offers some examples of Jesus' continuing physical nature and therefore his humanity after his resurrection.

> *Suddenly, Jesus was standing there among them! "Peace be with you," he said.* John 20:19b

> *The he said to Thomas, "Put your finger here, and look at my hands. Put your hand into the wound in my side. Don't be faithless any longer. Believe!"* John 20:27

> *Then Jesus served them the bread and the fish.* John 21:13

> *As they sat down to eat, he took the bread and blessed it. Then he broke it and gave it to them.* Luke 24:30

> *Then he breathed on them and said, "Receive the Holy Spirit."* John 20:22

After his resurrection, Jesus was seen by several people. He spoke to them, breathed on them, showed them his wounds from the crucifixion, broke bread (not figuratively, but actually broke the bread), and served his companions food. These are observations by many people, eyewitnesses, in the physical realm of a physical Jesus. Jesus was physical even after his resurrection. He provides us a glimpse into our own future of what we're promised after our resurrection.

He will take our weak mortal bodies and change them into glorious bodies like his own, using the same power with which he will bring everything under his control. Philippians 3:21

Jesus knows our struggles. He knows hunger and thirst. Being tired and weary were familiar feelings to Jesus. And he ultimately experienced excruciating physical pain during the beatings leading up to and the ultimate physical death on the cross. Yes, Jesus died a physical death. He knows what that's like. He did it so we have hope. Unless Jesus returns in our lifetime (a possibility), we will each meet the same end in this life. He gives us the hope and promise that once we die our physical death we will follow him into eternity. Our bodies will be raised and renewed and we'll live with him forever. Amen!

STUDY QUESTIONS

1. What is it about meals and the sharing of food that bring people together?

2. How can physical suffering bring people closer to God?

3. Why do you think it was important for Jesus to be physical, in the flesh?

4. What motivates you to care for and improve your physical body? If you focus on this too much, what can be the consequence?

5. When was a time that your physicalness drew you closer to God?

amazed

JESUS
HONORED HIS MOTHER

The next day there was a wedding celebration in the village of Cana in Gal-ilee. Jesus' mother was there, and Jesus and his disciples were also invited to the celebration. The wine supply ran out during the festivities, so Jesus' mother told him, "They have no more wine." "Dear woman, that's not our problem," Jesus replied. "My time has not yet come." But his mother told the servants, "Do whatever he tells you." John 2:1-5

M other's Day has been a long-standing tradition since early in the twentieth century. What began as a movement by a single woman to honor her recently deceased mother has become a holiday celebrated in many countries around the world.

Flowers are purchased. Cards are either bought or made by hand using crayons or colored markers. Banners are created. Breakfast is served in bed. All the traditions of this holiday honor the one who labored to bring us into this world.

So what's the big deal with celebrating mothers? And did Jesus in his humanity actually honor his mother? This chapter will look at two instances in which Jesus honoring his mother might have been part of his motive for action. But first, a few passages in which it seems Jesus did *not* honor his parents.

THE BOY JESUS

Luke 2 tells the story when Jesus was twelve years old and his parents made their annual trip to Jerusalem for the Passover festival. When the celebration was over, his parents, and presumably a whole pack of other people, left to head home. Jesus wasn't missed at first, but later that evening he turned up missing. His parents returned to the city to search for their son. It took three days, and to their relief, they finally found him. Where was he? Sitting in the temple discussing deep questions with the religious teachers. Jesus' mother responded as most mothers would, then or now. "Son!" she exclaimed. She called him out for causing such a panic.

> His parents didn't know what to think. "Son," his mother said to him, "why have you done this to us? Your father and I have been frantic, searching for you everywhere." "But why did you need to search?" he asked. "Didn't you know that I must be in my Father's house?" Luke 2:48–49

Jesus' response to his parents was curiously mature compared to what we'd consider typical for a twelve-year-old. "But why did you need to search?" he asked. "You should have known that I would be in my Father's house." His parents' response indicated they seemed not to know what he meant. Was Jesus misbehaving by not following his parents home?

Jewish tradition holds that a person may be viewed as an adult following his or her thirteenth birthday. There are other scriptural indications that imply that adulthood begins at age twenty. Charles Spurgeon, the well-renowned, nineteenth-century author and preacher, suggested that "a child of five can as truly be saved and regenerated as an adult."[1]

So rather than getting too hung up on exactly when a child passes into adulthood, it is commonly understood that the determination of adulthood had a different standard more than two thousand years ago. Could it be based on a combination of age and level of maturity that Jesus could be considered responsible for himself? His response to his parents indicated he was not a common twelve-year-old.

Another possibility could be that Jesus placed his priorities on his heavenly Father and his teachings above the authority of his earthly parents. We find in much of Jesus' teachings that he's big on choosing and setting priorities for what matters most. So, was Jesus dishonoring his parents? I don't think so. As a mature twelve-year-old having reached an age of accountability, it seems Jesus was simply following his heavenly Father's instructions.

WAS JESUS A FAMILY MAN?

Jesus was carrying on his normal activities—teaching and healing. A couple of guys, actually one was a teacher of religious law and the other was called a disciple, ended up in a briefly recorded conversation. They both claimed they wanted to join his movement. Jesus warned them that it was tough to do so. The second man asked if he could return home to bury his father then join in the ministry. Jesus rebuked him, instructing him to choose *now* what path to follow.

> *Another of his disciples said, "Lord, first let me return home and bury my father." But Jesus told him, "Follow me now. Let the spiritually dead bury their own dead."* **Matthew 8:21-22**

Was Jesus insensitive to not let the man return home to bury his dad?

Dr. David H. Stern is an author, messianic Jew, and a recognized authority on historical Jewish practices and tradition. Stern's perspective is that the man would not have been traveling with Jesus if his father were already dead. He might have been anticipating his death, but that it was unlikely he had already passed. His returning home would have assured him of his inheritance and, upon the receipt of his father's wealth, the man would be willing to return to follow Jesus.[2]

Jesus might have had this insight and known this man's actual motives. Jesus might have know that this man would be putting the prospect of physical pleasure and the security of receiving his father's wealth ahead of a life of following the Son of Man. Oftentimes trust in Jesus comes at a price. In this case, the man's sense of security was misplaced in his father's money.

Was this a cold, hard comment by Jesus then? Hardly, unless you consider the adage "the truth hurts." Seemingly harsh but true words by Jesus in this instance.

Additional stories in the gospels of Mark and Luke also describe situations where Jesus called those involved to make a tough choice. In Mark's story, Jesus' mother and siblings arrived while he was teaching. They sent word to him to come out and talk. The topic of the conversation they wished to have with Jesus is not recorded. When Jesus was told his family was waiting for him outside, he offered a surprising question.

> *Then Jesus' mother and brothers came to see him. They stood outside and sent word for him to come out and talk with them. There was a crowd sitting around Jesus, and someone said, "Your mother and your brothers are outside, asking for you." Jesus replied, "Who is my mother? Who are my brothers?"* Mark 3:31–33

If that were seemingly critical and confusing enough, Jesus then stated that anyone doing God's will were his siblings and mother.

> *Then he looked at those around him and said, "Look, these are my mother and brothers."* Mark 3:34

An instance in Luke 14 can also be seen as Jesus being a bit cold and harsh on family. He stated to a crowd that was following him that we must "hate" (in certain translations) our entire family—father, mother, wife, and children—if we desire to follow him.

> *"If you want to be my disciple, you must hate everyone else by comparison—your father and mother, wife and children, brothers and sisters—yes, even your own life. Otherwise, you cannot be my disciple."* Luke 14:26

The word we translate as "hate" from the original Greek text to English isn't the hate we understand. Strong's Concordance clarifies this term as to "love less in comparison."[3] We use the word *hate* as an absolute such as "I hate exercise" or "I hate vegetables" (yes, these are my issues I'm working through). The meaning of this is clear. I don't want to eat *any* vegetables or do *any* exercise. I'm not comparing vegetables to ice cream (which I do love to eat). So as I state this in English, "hating" vegetables is only a statement about vegetables and not relative to anything else. It's an absolute. I hate vegetables. Period.

Jesus asks only one thing from us. He wants our all. He isn't going to play second fiddle to anyone or anything. Can we love our mothers, our family, being in nature, golf, or anything else? Sure, he's saying we can love other things. But when the hard choices come, where the rubber meets the road, he calls us to choose him. And when we are confronted with these choices from time to time in our lives, it can be agonizing to follow Jesus and let go of the things of this life. Consider the previous accounts. We seem naturally drawn to things that bring us short-term comfort, pleasure, and security. So, we're called here to consider the previous accounts and make our choice. Choose Jesus or choose the way the rest of the world operates. Short term versus long term. Actually, the longest term.

THE WEDDING WINE

Jesus' mother was an invited guest to a wedding. Weddings were a multiday event during the time. The wine supply ran out, and Mary stated the problem to Jesus. "They have no more wine," she told him. Notice Mary didn't tell Jesus what to do, she simply alerted him of the problem. This left Jesus with a decision, his decision, of how to respond to the dilemma.

Jesus seemed to push back a bit. "Dear woman, that's not our problem, . . . My time has not yet come." Again, Mary didn't attempt to direct Jesus' actions, but did direct the servants: "Do whatever he tells you."

Then Jesus performed what is the commonly known miracle of turning water into wine. The six stone water jars, previously containing H_2O, now were brimming over with wine. Why did Jesus do this?

His motives are not recorded. I do think it's curious that after his initial resistance, Jesus actually seemed to reconsider his position on the matter. If he followed through with his initial response, Jesus would have allowed the ceremony to continue without wine, a serious downer for the event. Instead, he seemed to understand his mother's concern then chose to act rather than allow the wedding celebration to end on a sour note.

How many times are we asked to do something and initially bristle in our response? And when it's not on our agenda or is an inconvenience, it's tough sledding to overcome our original objection. So, does it seem possible that Jesus examined the situation, considered his mother's request, and decided the right cause of action was to follow through on what she implied she'd like him to do? To use this event as his means of launching his ministry? Of setting the events in motion that would bring an end to his physical life and provide for our eternal life? This could also be a great example of honoring a mother's request and placing her in high esteem.

HONOR FROM THE CROSS

The final account of Jesus honoring his mother is one of his final, earthly actions as a man in the flesh.

When Jesus saw his mother standing there beside the disciple he loved, he said to her, "Dear woman, here is your son." And he said to this disciple, "Here is your mother." And from then on this disciple took her into his home. John 19:26–27

Jesus had been beaten, ridiculed, and tortured. As he hung nailed to the cross, which shortly brought his death, he looked down and saw his mother standing beside his friend and disciple John. He said to his mother, "Woman, here is your son." And he said to John, "Here is your mother." Why did Jesus say this to them when clearly Mary was not John's mother?

In biblical times a woman alone without someone to care for her could be left to beg for her living. It would be a terrible existence. Since Joseph, Mary's husband and Jesus' earthly father wasn't mentioned, he might have already passed away. This would leave Jesus to be in charge of the family as the eldest son.

Jesus knew he wasn't long for this earth, and he wanted to ensure that his mother would be cared for, rather than leave her as a widow without a first-born son in the picture. So he gave over her care to John.

Can you imagine such a selfless act? Of all the things to be concerned about while dying and in great pain, Jesus honored his mother by assigning a caretaker for her. This is simply a wonderful and awe-inspiring act of compassion and selflessness.

We've all heard of the Ten Commandments that were given by God to Moses after he delivered the people out of slavery from Egypt. The fifth of these commandments is the first one that directs our dealings with people other than God.

"Honor your father and mother." Then you will live a long, full life in the land the Lord your God is giving you." Exodus 20:12

In Ephesians chapter 6, the apostle Paul expands on this topic.

"Honor your father and mother." This is the first commandment with a promise: If you honor your father and mother, "things will go well for you, and you will have a long life on the earth." **Ephesians 6:2–3**

Paul is referring to the place in scripture where God delivered the Ten Commandments to Moses. Within that Exodus text, God says more about some of the commandments than others. In the case of honoring our parents, God provides the promise referred to by Paul—in that living a life that honors our parents, God will provide us with a long and blessed life.

So what does this mean to us? How do we put this into practice today? Is this a message to children? Parents would hope so, but the original message was delivered to the Israelites who had just escaped the Pharaoh's grip on them, holding them in slavery in Egypt. They were adults, being told by God as a direct order to honor their parents.

Jesus not only honored his mother, he actually taught on the subject. He was in Jerusalem, and some of the Pharisees and other religious law teachers showed up. This was one of the many situations in which they tried to entrap Jesus into saying or doing something they defined as wrong. They were trying to take Jesus to task on why his disciples didn't perform the ceremonial handwashing before they ate a meal.

Jesus brought up compliance to tradition and laws to another, higher level.

Jesus replied, "And why do you, by your traditions, violate the direct commandments of God? For instance, God says, 'Honor your father and mother,' and 'Anyone who speaks disrespectfully of father or mother must be put to death.'" **Matthew 15:3–4**

We haven't all had great parents. Maybe one of your parents has been missing from your life because of mistakes made, a divorce, or, worse yet, some form of abuse. So this may be a difficult subject. If one of these things or something else traumatic happened in your childhood,

I know it may not mean much coming from me, but I'm very sorry. But the actions of parents do not discharge children from their responsibilities. And God laid these out clearly both to the Israelites in the Exodus story and in Jesus' teachings, and therefore to us in following the model of the earthly life Jesus led.

Here is an analogy about honoring someone or something that we might find difficult. In the military, a salute is required in situations when one encounters a superior officer. It's a sign of honor and respect. The superior officer wearing the uniform may be someone you know well. You might even dislike this person a great deal. But this does not allow you to shirk your responsibility of honoring and respecting that person enough to not salute them. You salute the uniform, not necessarily the person, because it's your job.

Honoring your parents will take on a variety of different forms throughout your lifetime, depending on your age and relationship. It might mean taking time to help with something. Being present at special occasions. Making a phone call or sending a message indicating that you're thinking about them. Taking care of something they need like running an errand. Near the end of their lives, it might mean helping with living arrangements or perhaps taking them in to live with you. Maybe allowing them to have something their way instead of what you think might be best for them.

One of the common themes related to honoring parents is the element of time. Time is the currency in relationships. Sure, time can be spent unproductively or unwisely. But we all have hardwired into us the value that time provides—it is a nonrenewable resource. No matter how much money you have, the playing field is level when it comes to time. We each get the same twenty-four hours each day. That's it.

So it's simply understood that when time is spent with another, that person knows that you've given them something of value—something that you can't get back, something that can't be spent another way or doing something else. You chose to spend it on them. And that's valuable. That's love.

However we do it, however it looks or is carried out, giving time to parents is the most valuable thing we can provide and is a great way to honor them and honor God by keeping his commandment.

Honor your mother. Honor your father. Jesus as God doesn't need to honor anyone. We are to honor him with all that we have, all that we are. Our very existence is always and only because of him. He deserves *our* honor. Yet he chose to honor his mother. He didn't have to. But in his humanity, Jesus set the standard for how we are to treat our parents. Honor your mother and father.

STUDY QUESTIONS

1. How did you celebrate Mother's Day and Father's Day as a child? Do you have any traditions with your children?

2. What situations have you been in where tough love and doing the right thing was needed?

3. What was your initial reaction to Jesus' tough words in family situations? How has your thinking changed after reading this chapter?

4. What are some ideas for honoring aging, adult parents once we're adults? How important is this, and what do we gain from doing this?

5. Why do you think Jesus honored his mother, even though as God he doesn't need to honor anyone?

JESUS
WAS TEMPTED

Then Jesus was led by the Spirit into the wilderness to be tempted there by the devil. Matthew 4:1

B y Matthew's account, Jesus had just been baptized, the heavens opened up, and the Spirit of God descended on him like a dove. A voice from heaven said, "This is my dearly loved Son, who brings me great joy" (Matthew 3:17). Then, and it does actually say "then" in the very next verse, Jesus was led out to the wilderness by the Holy Spirit to be tempted by none other than the prince of darkness himself. Does this mean that right after his baptism the temptation episode began? Scripture seems to imply that; it certainly can be taken that way. In any case, there is nothing else recorded between Jesus' baptism and his encounter with Satan in the desert. Luke's account is similar to Matthew's.

33

*Then Jesus, full of the Holy Spirit, returned from the Jordan River.
He was led by the Spirit in the wilderness, where he was tempted
by the devil for forty days. Jesus ate nothing all that time and
became very hungry.* Luke 4:1–2

First, for forty days and nights Jesus went without food. This would
bring many of us to be tempted by nearly anything, especially a fa-
vorite food. I can only imagine how weak and vulnerable I would be
when not having eaten any food for that long. Then the devil was on
the scene and pointed out that if Jesus was actually the Son of God,
he could change the stones into bread. Jesus refused and quoted from
scripture that people need more than simply food.

*People do not live by bread alone; rather, we live by every word
that comes from the mouth of the Lord.* Deuteronomy 8:3b

Next, Satan took Jesus to Jerusalem to the highest point of the temple
and tempted him to jump. Not only this, but the evil one tried to use
God's own word against Jesus quoting scripture. "He will order his
angels to protect you. . . . They will hold you up with their hands so
you won't even hurt your foot on a stone" (Psalm 91:11–12). Jesus' response says we are not to test God.

*You must not test the Lord your God as you did when you com-
plained at Massah.* Deuteronomy 6:16

Isn't it interesting that the devil quoted God's word in an attempt to
use that against Jesus? The evil one will go to any length to trip us up
in life, even allowing us to find single scripture verses that he'll twist
in such a way that it fits a personal agenda leading us down the wrong
path. James addresses this by noting:

*You say you have faith, for you believe that there is one God. Good
for you! Even the demons believe this, and they tremble in terror.*
James 2:19

So *believe* is one thing; that even Satan does. But *follow* is what we're additionally called to do. Jesus asked this of us. This differentiates us from Satan, the demons, or anyone else that would claim to believe, but believe only and not follow.

Finally, the devil took Jesus to the peak of a mountain and showed him the world. Satan's promise was to give it all to Jesus if he would kneel down and worship him. Jesus told him to scram and again quoted God's word that we are to worship and serve God alone.

> *"You must fear the Lord your God and serve him."*
> **Deuteronomy 6:13a**

Of all the things Jesus was and experienced in his humanity, this might be the most important. He lived as a man, as physical as we are, was tempted, just as you and I are, but stood up to the tests and did so without sin.

Bruce Ware, the author of *The Man Christ Jesus: Theological Reflections on the Humanity of Christ* has this to say on the temptation of Jesus: "'God cannot be tempted by evil' (James 1:13). But Jesus was tempted. In fact, Hebrews tells us that he was 'tempted as we are, yet without sin' (Heb. 4:15). So the temptations of Jesus relate directly to his humanity, to be sure. But we also must take full account of the fact that in addition to being fully human, Jesus was fully God."[1]

Let's attempt to settle a couple of things before we get much further. Is temptation sin? And if it is, did Jesus sin?

The author of Hebrews puts this to rest for us. In Hebrews 4, the author refers to these events and notes that Jesus understands us and our weaknesses because he faced them as we do. Just to be clear, being tempted is not sin. We are confronted with temptations to choose to do something or not do something that will stand squarely in the way of our full relationship with our Father. Acting on the choice for which we are tempted *is* sin. Being tempted is not sin. Jesus did not sin. Jesus was tempted. Again, temptation is not sin.

> *This High Priest of ours understands our weaknesses, for he faced all of the same testings we do, yet he did not sin.* **Hebrews 4:15**

The High Priest referred to is clarified earlier as Jesus. Jesus understands and experienced temptation as we do and did not sin.

Let's examine each of the three temptations separately. Within these challenges laid by the devil before Jesus, there are lessons that we can apply to our daily lives.

WILL GOD MEET MY BASIC NEEDS?

Jesus was forty days without food and the devil tempted him to convert the stones to bread to satisfy his appetite, which must have been massive by this time. This could be seen as a temptation to not trust God to meet our physical needs.

> *"He gave you water from the rock! He fed you with manna in the wilderness, a food unknown to your ancestors. He did this to humble you and test you for your own good."* **Deuteronomy 8:15b–16**

After the Exodus of the Israelites from Egyptian slavery, they wandered the desert for forty years. There's that number "forty" again, the same length of time Jesus spent in the desert being tempted. In Deuteronomy 8, Moses recalled this, how God led them into the wilderness for forty years, humbled them by letting them go hungry to test their character, and then feeding them with the food (manna) to meet their physical needs. Throughout the Old Testament, the Israelites struggled to fully submit to God and trust him, even after he showed himself trustworthy through his many interventions in their lives and through the provisions he generously supplied.

Sounds like they struggled with that, like I do now.

It seems time and time again, the first thing I do in the face of a challenge when my needs (and sometimes wants) aren't going to be met, I push the panic button. I jump into self-preservation mode and do all I can to prevent any sort of loss of my quality of life. So does this mean I should just pray and wait? Sometimes, yes, that may be what I'm supposed to do. And in many cases we see in the Bible there are examples of people who took God-directed action. So I rely on God for his direction and act according to that. In any case, when I allow God to do his work in my life, there's always something in it for me, even if it's a lesson I didn't know I needed to learn. He's in it for my good. My job is to trust him and believe he is out for my good.

Sometimes this means I may not be returned to my previous state. That's the tough part for most of us. Acceptance of the place God leads us into, if that's his will, can be very difficult.

Where the Israelites failed, Jesus succeeded. More than fourteen hundred years earlier, the former slaves who were brought to their freedom by a loving and powerful God couldn't see to trust him for their basic needs. Jesus, a man also in a desert, starved and alone, passed that test.

WILL HARM COME TO ME?

The second temptation is similar to hunger in that it is the meeting of a physical need for safety. Will God keep us safe?

Satan takes Jesus to the highest point of the temple and urges him to jump. He further taunts him to do so only *if* he is the Son of God. If this isn't enough of a challenge, the devil uses God's own word in an attempt to make his case. Satan quotes Psalm 91:11–12, that God will send his angels to protect him when he jumps.

Have you ever had your authenticity challenged? Want to be sure you look good in a situation? To be sure that others know who you are and that you're somebody? I hope I'm not alone in this, because this is something I've struggled with for much of my life. Early in my business career, I was constantly insecure and felt I needed to prove myself. Even though I had a title and was granted authority by company management to carry out certain tasks and objectives, I would still be sure that my fingerprints were on everything. I would look for the glory, sometimes trampling others in the process. If one of the folks

I did this to is reading this now and saying, "Yup, he sure did that," I must say I'm sorry.

Another button Satan is attempting to push with Jesus is to get him to manipulate God into action to save him rather than trusting God's word and his promises. How often do we test God like this? Ever prayed, "God, if *fill in the blank*, then I will *fill in blank with the bargain you offered*." Or maybe it's a sense that things aren't fair; you're a good person, trying your best, and yet others, people that aren't as good in your eyes (maybe not even trying to follow Jesus!) get all the good fortune in life.

The author of Hebrews used the mistrust of the Israelites in the wilderness as a way to warn the present-day Jews to not repeat their mistrust and test God's patience. In the fourth chapter we find the comparison set up. It says anyone who disobeys and mistrusts God, as the Israelites did while in the wilderness, will fail to get into God's eternal rest.

> *God's promise of entering his rest still stands, so we ought to tremble with fear that some of you might fail to experience it. For this good news—that God has prepared this rest—has been announced to us just as it was to them. But it did them no good because they didn't share the faith of those who listened to God.*
> Hebrews 4:1–2

God is not into making bargains. He demands and deserves our trust. My problem is giving him my complete trust and having too short a view, thinking less of eternity and more about my present circumstances. I want what I want when I want it. I sometimes make my faith a condition of God's response. I don't see the response I want; my faith waivers.

Faith, trust, and following Jesus does not necessarily mean we will be rescued from our current, temporal, and perhaps difficult circumstances. Sometimes God intervenes, shows us his power, and heals someone with cancer. God will deliver someone at just the right time to avert a devastating situation. He will provide a financial gift to get us out of a jam just in the nick of time when there seemed to be no hope or way out.

Or, he may not.

As unpleasant as this is, each of us will come to the same end on this planet. Our physical bodies will perish. Yes, die. Unless we survive until the time Jesus returns, no matter our economic situation, worldly success, size of our home, or other accomplishments, at some point our bodies will fail, and we will face inevitable physical death.

God is far more concerned about our character than our comfort. It's not that he's unconcerned about our comfort, but he has his priorities. He has his sights set on the long term. He has a great reward in store that is unique for each of us. This life is our great test. We each have our own circumstances, and in the crucible of this life, God will use all of these as the means to forge our character for his purposes and to ultimately bring us into his kingdom.

By the way, it is commonly believed that most of the original apostles, the men who lived with Jesus and experienced a loving, first-hand relationship with him, died violent deaths because of their faith. God allowed Jesus' chosen followers, friends, and companions to Jesus during his earthly ministry to die violent painful deaths. So will he allow there to be discomfort and difficulties in our life? Almost certainly.

I WANT IT. I NEED IT.

The last temptation was one we can easily relate to today. Lust, greed, and power.

On top of a mountain, Satan showed Jesus the whole world and offered to put Jesus in charge if only he knelt down to worship him. You see, Jesus came to rule the world. His people of that time, the Jews, were oppressed by Roman rule in their own land, including the city of Jerusalem. To be made king and accept the offer to have the ability to change all this, would be tempting. It would also be shortsighted.

We saw this play out in the life of Judas, the disciple that later betrayed Jesus. A woman was anointing Jesus with expensive perfume during supper. Judas rightfully pointed out the high value of the fragrance and that it could be sold and the money given to the poor. As the saying goes, Judas was generally right and specifically wrong. Judas was looking at the short term. Jesus accepted the gift, given in love and admiration by the woman as her act of worship. Jesus was looking at the long term, the woman's heart.

> *But Judas Iscariot, the disciple who would soon betray him, said, "That perfume was worth a year's wages. It should have been sold and the money given to the poor."* John 12:4-5

Tom Petters was a rising star in the business world in the late twentieth century. Not only was he successful, he was generous. He gave millions of dollars to charities and schools for their betterment. Only one problem. It wasn't his money. Not really. Petters operated a Ponzi scheme, growing his wealth in a deceitful fashion at the great expense of those who trusted him. The shortsighted scheme came to its inevitable end. Petters is now in prison, and the government has been working to restore his investors and debtors with funds owed by clawing back monies donated to these same charities. So short term, Petters was helping these institutions, while long term, he actually harmed some of them.

God will reconcile and make all things right in the end. In the Petters' case, only some of those owed will be made whole again. For God's judgment, all things will be made right. Jesus passed the test and did not succumb to the temptation of greed or power. Jesus has the long-term view squarely in his sights.

> *I heard a loud shout from the throne, saying, "Look, God's home is now among his people! He will live with them, and they will be his people. God himself will be with them. He will wipe every tear from their eyes, and there will be no more death or sorrow or crying or pain. All these things are gone forever."* Revelation 21:3-4

The great twentieth-century pastor and expositor, Ray Stedman, aptly pointed out that "as Jesus says, it is not our circumstances, but some weakness within, some allurement to which we yield, some inner urge."[2] The temptation is in us and is our nature. Jesus was alone in the wilderness. He had no one to blame, and he couldn't claim that he was coerced. We'd often rather blame the situation or someone else. There is no doubt that there are "slippery places" where temptation is great. But Jesus showed that even in the absence of this, temptation occurs and is caused only by Satan. God never tempts us.

> *And remember, when you are being tempted, do not say, "God is tempting me." God is never tempted to do wrong, and he never tempts anyone else. Temptation comes from our own desires, which entice us and drag us away.* James 1:13–14

Jesus stood up to temptation. He showed in his humanity that it can be done. Even while being physically weak, having the desire to connect with the Father in a loving relationship, and having the agenda of saving us from destruction, Jesus faced down each temptation, took the long view, honored God, and became our Savior.

Jesus had the Holy Spirit on his side to help him, encourage him, and comfort him while facing great temptation. So do we.

Study questions

1. How good (or poor) is your judgment when you are very hungry or over tired? Can you mention a time that you did something that you might not have done if you'd been physically stronger?

2. When have you felt that God's word (either by you or someone else) has been taken out of context to fit a situation? How can we test the correctness of the use of scripture?

3. When was a time you had your basic needs threatened (shelter, food, clothing) and you needed to rely on God (perhaps delivered through other people) to help you out? How did you feel in that situation?

4. Tell of when God provided for your physical safety.

5. Note a time when you lusted over a prized possession. Did you get it? If so, how did that feel? Did the feeling last?

CHAPTER FOUR

JESUS
SUBMITTED

Though he was God, he did not think of equality with God as something to cling to. **Philippians 2:6**

The relationship between God the Father, Jesus the Son, and the Holy Spirit as a three-in-one God has been considered for ages. I won't attempt to unpack that mystery in this text, except to consider this: Jesus as God, surrendered his authority, became a man, and regularly submitted to the Father—and did this for our benefit.

The apostle Paul suggests in his letter to the Philippians that our attitude is to be that of Jesus' attitude—one of humility. Jesus voluntarily came to earth and subjected himself to a human life, one that was filled with all the same challenges that we face today. He didn't need to do this, but he wanted to so he did. He did this so that we might live. His sacrifice ensured this.

BREAKING THE SABBATH RULES

On several occasions during Jesus' earthly ministry, he broke the Sabbath rules that were set up and enforced by the Jewish leaders—at least the laws were violated in the eyes of those Jewish leaders. On one occasion recorded in John 5, Jesus found a man who was lame near a pool around which the sick gathered in hope of becoming well. Jesus asked the man if he wanted to become well. The man believed in the healing power of the pool and didn't know to whom he was speaking. "I can't, sir," said the man. He believed he had to reach the pool before anyone else did, when the water was just beginning to stir. It was understood that the first person in the pool at that time, when the water was stirred, would be healed. As this man was unable to walk without physical assistance, he would not make it to the pool in time. So the man watched as others moved into the pool ahead of him as he had done for the past thirty-eight years.

Jesus told the man, "Stand up, pick up your mat, and walk!" (John 5:8). The man was healed on the spot. He took up his mat and walked away. Apparently there were Jewish leaders within sight. They pointed out to the man that it was illegal for him to carry his mat on the Sabbath. This was paramount to working, which was against their rules. The man who was previously paralyzed said he was told to pick up the mat and walk by the man who healed him. Jesus had slipped away into the crowd previously, so he wasn't found immediately.

Later Jesus was confronted by the same men who had harassed the man who was lame, and they insisted that Jesus broke the Sabbath rules. Jesus said, "My Father is always working, and so am I" (John 5:17). This infuriated the leaders as now Jesus not only broke their rules but he compared himself to God, a serious offense. Then, Jesus made a statement that set the relationship between him and the Father in order.

> So Jesus explained, "I tell you the truth, the Son can do nothing by himself. He does only what he sees the Father doing. Whatever the Father does, the Son also does." John 5:19

Jesus does only what the Father does. No more, no less. He saw the Father work in creation of the heavens and earth, so he worked in creation to disciple, teach, and draw people to himself. He saw the Father show mercy to the Israelites and rescue them from the Egyptian slavery. Jesus in turn relieved the man by the pool of his paralysis and urged him to turn his life around. He patterned his life, actions, and choices after what he saw the Father do. In this way, Jesus gave up his will and does only, and the verse does say "only," what the Father does.

TEACHING IN THE TEMPLE

Jesus snuck into Judea for a festival being held there. He tried to stay out of sight of the Jewish leaders as he was attracting their scrutiny. Then halfway through the celebration, Jesus headed up to the temple and started to teach. Believing that Jesus wasn't as well studied as they were, the Jewish leaders questioned how it was that he knew so much about scripture.

> *So Jesus told them, "My message is not my own; it comes from God who sent me."* John 7:16

Jesus pointed out that those presenting their own ideas were only looking for praise for themselves. But when you seek to honor the one who sent you, the message he has is what you present. Jesus was making the distinction that the Father sent him, and he was teaching the Father's ideas and message, not his own.

It would have been easy for Jesus to claim the message to be his own. He had built quite a reputation for being a miracle worker. By this point, it is recorded that Jesus turned water into wine at the wedding at Cana, healed both the Capernaum official's son and the man who was lame, fed five thousand people near the Sea of Galilee, and walked across a lake during a storm. If anyone during the period could have established the authority to teach and advance his own ideas, it would have been Jesus.

But this wasn't Jesus' way. He was satisfied delivering the message the Father provided. He wasn't out to attract attention or advance his own agenda. He wasn't seeking praise for himself but for his Father in heaven. Jesus didn't want to be honored but only wanted to point to the one he honored. Jesus was perfect in both teaching his Father's message with authority and yet remaining humble as a servant in the process. He set the example for us in his humility and deference to the Father's will.

REMAIN IN MY LOVE

The gospel of John records several messages and instructions Jesus gave his closest followers near the end of his earthly ministry. Reading the chapters of John 14–17 is like being a fly on the wall listening to Jesus give his final directions as well as express his love and affection for the disciples. It's such an intimate conversation in which Jesus changed the order of things by calling them his friends rather than servants, as he had now given them complete instructions from the Father. Jesus called them as chosen (John 6:70).

Jesus used the metaphor of a vine. He is the vine; the Father is the gardener. The gardener prunes the branches not bearing fruit. The disciples had already been pruned and were now ready to carry on without Jesus' physical presence with them. Jesus urged the disciples to remain connected to him, as a vine branch needs to be connected to the vine in order to produce fruit. We can't bear fruit on our own.

He said his love for them was just as the Father's love was for himself, and that they were to remain in his love. How to do that? How to remain in his love? Jesus explained.

> *"When you obey my commandments, you remain in my love, just as I obey my Father's commandments and remain in his love."*
> John 15:10

Love. It seems we want this more than about anything else. We do crazy, irrational things for love when we are attempting to develop a romantic relationship. And love carries us through challenges in relationships, provides the stick-to-it-ness required to be a parent, and is arguably the force behind all well-meaning, unselfish acts of generosity and bravery.

The love Jesus describes is unconditional but comes with an expectation and a promise. The expectation is our obedience. That's how we find his love—through our obedience. As we follow Jesus, his ways, and his teachings, and give more of ourselves over to him, we remain in his love.

I believed in Jesus for a while before I committed to serve him. A pinnacle moment in my life of beginning to follow Jesus was when I began to show up for a breakfast ministry at a local homeless shelter. The day begins at 4:30 a.m. by hauling cooking implements and groceries across the street to cook in the kitchen. After nearly an hour of preparation, we're ready to serve until 6:30 a.m. Then cleanup begins, ending around 7:00 a.m. It's a wonderful program that provides a meal for those in need as well as opportunities to connect and build relationships with the residents. Since joining this ministry regularly, my life began to change dramatically. My desire to know Jesus grew, and important relationships in my life began to flourish. I felt called to this ministry and became obedient to Jesus in this, and his love has been poured out into my life.

"I have told you these things so that you will be filled with my joy. Yes, your joy will overflow!" John 15:11

That's the promise. Jesus lived a life of obedience to the Father. He then instructs us to obey him, and when we do he will fill us with his joy. That's his joy, the best kind of joy—endless, pure, and unquenchable joy. Jesus also urges us to love others in the same way he loves us.

Follow him as he followed the Father. Obey him as he obeyed the Father. Jesus will pour out his joy into us. We are to use this joy to fuel our love for others.

MEDDLING MOTHER

The mother of James and John made a peculiar request of Jesus. She must have really believed he was who he said he was, as she acknowledged his future kingdom. Did she believe this was an earthly kingdom? It's not clear, but she clearly seemed to believe Jesus was going to be a ruler of some kind.

She knelt before Jesus and made a request.

> *She replied, "In your Kingdom, please let my two sons sit in places of honor next to you, one at your right and the other on your left."*
> **Matthew 20:21b**

Jesus replied that she didn't know what she was asking. The mother obviously didn't have the benefit of knowing the future suffering and death Jesus would experience. Knowing his own future, Jesus challenged the brothers and asked if they'd be willing to join in his suffering. "Oh yes," said the siblings. Jesus then foreshadowed that their lives would be replete with sorrow and suffering. He then clarified the order of things as to who determines the places in his throne room.

> *"But I have no right to say who will sit on my right or my left. My Father has prepared those places for the ones he has chosen."*
> **Matthew 20:23b**

Jesus knew the order of things. He deferred to the Father at all times. He bent to his Father's will perfectly and set the example for us. As for the eternal pairing next to his throne of honor, Jesus suspended his own will and submitted to the Father.

THE BITTER CUP

Perhaps the best-known example of Jesus' compliance to the Father's will is during his prayer in the garden of Gethsemane. In the evening prior to his arrest, Jesus, along with Peter, James, and John, headed out to pray. He left the others for a time of solitude with his heavenly

Father to petition him regarding the events that were about to come. In this, we see a glimpse into Jesus' thoughts as he asked his Father if there was another way to accomplish the mission set before him. He came to Earth in human form for one reason: to save us from sin. Because God is God, he could do this in immeasurable ways. However it was through Jesus—coming as a man, bearing the punishment we deserve, and then raising himself from the dead to conquer Satan and his plan for our destruction. Jesus gives us a way out of this world through himself.

In one continuous recorded thought, Jesus asked if there was another way, and if not, he wanted his Father's will to be done and not his own.

He went on a little father and bowed with his face to the ground, praying, "My Father! If it is possible, let this cup of suffering be taken away from me. Yet I want your will to be done, not mine."
Matthew 26:39

Jesus set for us in this scene a pointed example of how we are to relate to the Father. Can you imagine? Jesus had full knowledge of what was about to happen in detail—every accusation; his persecutors spitting in his face; being slapped, punched, and stripped of his clothing; lashed with a whip, a crown of thrones pressed into the flesh and bone of his scalp; and then nailed to a cross and left to die an excruciating death. Yet he submitted to the Father. He agreed to follow his will and not his own.

I've suffered some loss in my life, as have most of us. I've endured financial challenges and relationship troubles. I've feared for my children and their choices, struggled with my own particular areas of sin in my life. As I've worked to bend my will to the Father's, I've learned to ask for what I want, then end my prayer with my agreement that I'll follow God's will, whatever that might be. But in no case, not once, have I had the foreknowledge of the challenges that lie ahead for me. God protects us from the future by revealing it to us one moment at a time. I can't imagine how much more difficult it would be to agree to what is about to happen in my life, especially when it's not to my immediate favor.

But Jesus did exactly that. Even though he knew the future events, which included physical torture, suffering, and death, he agreed to follow. In spite of the adversity, Jesus walked into it knowing it was his Father's will, so he agreed to abide in it. He set the example of how to follow God's will, even when the journey would be difficult. Jesus trusted God with his very life. God always honors our faithfulness. Not always in our time, but he always is faithful.

Can you look back at your life and see that some of the adversity turned out to be beneficial? The opportunity afforded us with age is in gaining wisdom. Not always, but sometime God seems to allow us to look back at a situation or series of events, and we can see how he knit these things together perfectly to place us just where he wanted us. Those situations might have been difficult in their present moment, might have represented some loss, or might even have been the result of a poor choice on our part. But when we follow Jesus, he will use all those things for his purpose.

> *And we know that God causes everything to work together for the good of those who love God and are called according to his purpose for them.* Romans 8:28

STUDY QUESTIONS

1. God worked for six days during the creation then set the example for rest on the seventh day. Why is it important to have a Sabbath?

2. What are the reason(s) it's important to give God credit and not take the accolades for yourself?

3. What did Jesus say about how to remain in his love? What do you get as the result of this?

4. How is it that you can suffer for Jesus today? What things are you willing to do to suffer for him?

5. Think of a time you prayed for God's will and didn't get the outcome you wanted. Were you able to see how God worked and/or blessed you in the end?

amazed

JESUS
GAVE NICKNAMES

James and John (the sons of Zebedee, but Jesus nicknamed them "Sons of Thunder"). Mark 3:17

Jack Nicklaus, the great American golfer, is known as "The Golden Bear," which describes both his physical appearance and his tenacity on the links. Babe Ruth, the baseball legend, was known as "The Sultan of Swat," a statement about his ability to hit home runs. Frank Sinatra was known as "Ol' Blue Eyes," which is obvious looking at a color head shot of him. And the famous gangster of the late twentieth century, John Gotti, was called "Teflon Don" for his stature with the mafia and his ability to evade prosecution by the law.

THROW IT DEEP, BUFF!

After high school, I joined the football team at the small college I first attended. The coach was a big guy with a short NFL career. He was a real man's man. Somehow, early in my experience at the college, my coach learned that I graduated from Buffalo High School in the town of the same name. From that moment on, he began to call me Buff. Since my last name also begins with the letter B, I wonder if there was some association between that and the nickname. Who knows?

From time to time in football practice, we would fool around with a few of our own plays that weren't in the playbook. One of them was the flanker option pass. This called for me to be positioned wide right in the flanker position (sorry for those of you that can't relate to this, so I'll try to get to the point shortly). The quarterback would take the snap from center; I would take one step forward and three back. The quarterback would throw me the ball, which was a lateral (a backward pass) making it legal for me to throw the ball downfield. I could then run, or better yet, throw the ball downfield to the tight end running up the seam. The play attempts to fool the defense because in football, you can't throw a second pass—unless the first pass wasn't a pass at all, because it was a backward or lateral pass.

So, we were ahead significantly in a game late in the season. The quarterback called our play in the huddle. It went off perfectly, at least to start. After I caught the ball, I turned to throw it downfield to the tight end. I was very near our sidelines with our coach only a few yards from me. As I took the ball back to throw it, from our sideline I heard the coach yell, "Buff, no!" The pass fell to the ground having missed the intended receiver. In the pressure of the game and in the midst of a gadget pass play, the only reference to who I was that came to the coach's mind was my nickname, Buff.

To conclude the story: Years later I was in downtown Minneapolis riding on an elevator heading down after being near the top of a high-rise for an appointment. The elevator stopped as more passengers got on. I instantly recognized one of the newcomers as a former member of the same college football team, who I hadn't seen since school. I exclaimed, "Scottie!" The man turned around, looked at me and said, "Hey, Buff, how are you?"

Nicknames have a certain stickiness, even to the point where, as was the case with Scottie (by the way, another nickname), my nickname was my identity. I'll bet not more than a handful of my former teammates actually know my given name. So, if any of those guys are reading this book right now, they may not even recognize they were part of this story!

NOT A NICKNAME

Nicknames can be a term of endearment or affection. Unfortunately they can also be a means of belittling or expressing contempt towards another.

A moniker is a form of a nickname. A shortening of a proper, full name or a variation of a name such as Rob or Bob for Robert, or Beth or Liz for Elizabeth are examples of monikers.

Sometimes nicknames express irony. A large man might be given the nickname Tiny or Slim, or a tall person could obtain the name Shorty. When irony is the motivation for the nickname, it's often received as humorous. The same nickname can also be hurtful when it is a statement of truth. Actually, there is an irony in that itself, isn't there?

It seems that men are significantly more prolific when handing out nicknames than are women. No disrespect intended here—sure there are Flo Jo and The Hollywood Madam—but if you search for nicknames, there are dozens of men that have nicknames for every one woman. Why is that?

WHY NICKNAMES?

Here's my take. Men are generally uncomfortable or even afraid of showing affection, especially when it comes to giving it or getting it from other men. One time my wife, Carla, went golfing with me and some of my pals. We spent four plus hours needling and picking on each other until the round was over. Carla stated to me afterwards, "You guys aren't very nice to each other." She seemed to think we actually meant what was said. I explained to her that if you're the guy in the group that *isn't* being picked on, you know you are not liked by the other guys.

I'm not here to justify this behavior. I know that there are times that picking on each other as guys can be detrimental. However, I am stating an observation I've seen over the years—that guys use mild sarcasm and pick on other guys as terms of endearment. And the giving of nicknames falls into this category.

I think this is a motivation for nicknames, at least the ones that aren't malicious or ill intended. If you've ever heard an interview with Tiger Woods, the great American golfer, you'll rarely hear him use a proper first name for any of his fellow players. For his comrades in golf, he has a nickname for every one of them.

Jesus lived as a man. As he was without sin, we can be confident in the assurance that his motives were pure in giving nicknames. And he did.

WHAT'S IN A NAME?

In Mark 3, there is a list of the twelve disciples Jesus chose to be his regular companions. It says he sent them out to preach and gave them the authority to cast out demons. As the list comes to the names James and John, it mentions their heritage (the sons of Zebedee) and then says something peculiar in parenthesis.

> *James and John (the sons of Zebedee, but Jesus nicknamed them "Sons of Thunder").* Mark 3:17

Did you catch that? Sons of Thunder? What a word picture that creates! These two guys were lifelong fishermen, as was their father. They likely grew up in the outdoors, spending hour after hour in the sun, on the water, hoisting up the fish-heavy nets into the boat. Their skin might have become dark and leathery from all the time in the sun. Their shoulders were probably broad and their biceps and forearms large from dealing with the weight of the fish-filled nets. I also image them with lots of hair on their arms, chests, and back. Perhaps both would be tall for the era: six feet or more. Think of the build of a modern-day football linebacker or defensive tackle. That's my picture of these guys.

As big guys and fishermen, they might not have been the gentlest of fellows. I wonder if they were a bit clumsy. They might have even liked to mix it up a bit when in a disagreement. Historically, career fishermen were known to be in a fight or two. And how about loud? I wonder if when they spoke, it was a few decibels beyond most others' speaking voices. If so, Jesus would find good use for this—grooming them to preach in public later.

FIERY TEMPERS

There is a gospel account of the time when the two brothers asked Jesus if they should call down fire from heaven to torch some villagers who refused to let them stay there. It seems the brothers were a couple of hot heads (pun intended).

> When James and John saw this, they said to Jesus, "Lord, should we call down fire from heaven to burn them up?" Luke 9:54

It's interesting that they believed they had the ability to call down fire from the sky to wipe out this town, and first asked Jesus permission to do so. They had enough faith in Jesus to believe that such things were possible, but didn't yet get the mission and purpose that Jesus set out for them. At least not yet.

> We know what real love is because Jesus gave up his life for us. So we also ought to give up our lives for our brothers and sisters. 1 John 3:16

James and John did eventually get the point. James is thought to be the first (or one of the first) apostles to be martyred for his faith. John is thought to have written the books in the New Testament named after him and possibly the book of Revelation. His writings contain more about the topic of love and Christ's love for us than most others. So these two knuckleheads—who earlier fought for their own personal ambitions and had hair-trigger tempers—were transformed by Jesus into courageous and loving followers of his.

WHY "SONS OF THUNDER"?

I recognize I'm taking some liberties with my earlier assessment of the brothers, but I really like the idea that Jesus gave nicknames and gave this one in particular. It gives us the opportunity to think beyond the brothers' given names and build an image in our minds that is far richer than simply James and John. Why did Jesus give this particular nickname? We don't know, but it might be that Jesus meant this as a term of affection for these two men that he tutored, trusted, lived with, traveled with, and loved during the short time of his recorded ministry. I think this could be an example of Jesus in his manhood, showing his affection to two men he clearly loved and doing so in a way that men understand.

Have you ever had a nickname? Ever given one to someone else? I hope that there was no harm intended or received from it. Nicknames are a wonderful way to cause us to create an image of another person and to develop a closeness that might not be developed in its absence.

Jesus is God and a man. I think it is very much a guy thing to give other guys nicknames. What nickname would Jesus give you?

STUDY QUESTIONS

1. Have you ever had a nickname? What was the origin or story behind it?

2. Why is it that men find it difficult to express affection? Do you think this is changing?

3. What could be the reasons Jesus called James and John "Sons of Thunder"?

4. Jesus called the apostle Peter this "rock I will build my church [on]" (Matthew 16:18). What do you think he meant by that?

5. What nickname might Jesus give to you? Why?

amazed

JESUS
WAS AMAZED

When Jesus heard this, he was amazed. Luke 7:9a

Jesus had just finished delivering a message to his followers and was returning to the city of Capernaum. Having heard of Jesus, a Roman officer sent some important Jewish leaders to Jesus to ask him to come and heal his dying slave. Jesus left for the officer's house, but just before his arrival, the officer sent some folks out to meet Jesus.

They delivered a message. They told Jesus not to bother to come all the way to the officer's house as the officer had said he was not worthy of that honor. However, they told Jesus the officer had said if Jesus just said the slave would be healed, the officer believed it would be done. They explained that he was in command of many soldiers who always do as he says. The officer believed Jesus had the same power over this sickness.

The next verse is a simple but rich and wonderful phrase that really caught me off guard while reading the gospels and trying to get to know Jesus in a deeper and more personal way.

When Jesus heard this, he was amazed. Matthew 8:10a

Amazed? Really? How can God be amazed?

SLAVERY IN THE BIBLE

The Bible includes many examples of slavery or of those being held to serve others without having full human rights. From the time of Moses with the Israelites being forced to serve the Egyptian Pharaoh to the time of Jesus and beyond, slavery is referred to frequently.

Caution is needed when considering the slave and master relationship in scripture. There is no doubt that slavery is never a good thing. However, we often look at this through a current lens and not through a perspective of the period. So to clear up the temptation to judge the Roman officer (centurion) too harshly because he had a slave in his charge, consider the following.

Slavery sometimes occurred as the result of the loss of a battle, and the losers would become servants to those having conquered them. So along with losing all their possessions and their homes, they would lose their freedom.

As you approach a town to attack it, you must first offer its people terms for peace. If they accept your terms and open the gates to you, then all the people inside will serve you in forced labor. Deuteronomy 20:10–11

A slave or bond servant was referred to in the New Testament with the Greek word *doulos*, which has been interpreted to mean a variety of service relationships between a servant and master. A bond servant could be one who voluntarily sells oneself into the service of another, perhaps to pay off a debt. Upon completion of the agreed upon service, the bond servant would be released from service.

"If you buy a Hebrew slave, he may serve for no more than six years. Set him free in the seventh year, and he will owe you nothing for his freedom." Exodus 21:2

Jesus compared himself to a slave when he explained why he washed the disciples' feet at the Last Supper. When he finished with the last pair of feet, he joined the disciples at dinner and used this example of how we are to treat others. He used the same term *doulos* as he described the serving relationship he just demonstrated.

After washing their feet, he put on his robe again and sat down and asked, "Do you understand what I was doing? You call me 'Teacher' and 'Lord,' and you are right, because that's what I am. And since I, your Lord and Teacher, have washed your feet, you ought to wash each other's feet. I have given you an example to follow. Do as I have done to you. I tell you the truth, slaves are not greater than their master. Nor is the messenger more important than the one who sends the message. Now that you know these things, God will bless you for doing them." John 13:12–17

There is a lot of discussion about slavery throughout scripture. Some of it is clearly an abuse of one's rights, and other situations are less clear. The interpretation of the term for slavery brings a variety of meanings, of which only some parallel what we might currently think of as slavery. This should not derail the importance of the lesson contained within this context.

SETTING THE SCENE

The process of being "amazed" involves surprise, wonder, or astonishment. The term used in the original Greek text is *ethaumasen,* which literally translates into English as the word *marvel.* Wonder and astonishment are considered synonyms for marvel. The implication here is that there is some sort of a surprise along with admiration, which creates in us a sense of wonder or astonishment or causes us to marvel at or about something.

Does is seem almost odd to you that God could be amazed? How is it possible to surprise someone that already knows everything? Everything that has happened, is happening, and is going to happen? Doesn't the process of surprise, a requirement for amazement, involve the lack of advanced knowledge? Confused? Let's back up a bit in the story.

A SOLDIER'S ROLE

The object of Jesus' amazement is the Roman officer. A Roman centurion (this man's title) was typically in charge of eighty to one hundred men with senior commanders in charge of even more. The Romans occupied the region where Jesus spent his life as a man, and the relationship with the Jewish people native to the area was fragile. The Jews did not welcome the Romans in Jerusalem and the surrounding areas. The Roman army and government worked with the Jewish leaders to maintain order of the local, Jewish people. A volatile situation to manage for sure.

Centurions were often physically good specimens. They were disciplined and enforced the same among those they commanded. First and foremost they were soldiers. And like all good soldiers, they took orders. They followed their command. They were never insubordinate. Imagine a big, burly, rule-abiding and rule-enforcing man. These guys did what they were told, didn't ask questions, and shouted "yes sir!" upon receiving a direct order. These were guys one didn't mess with.[1]

So imagine this Roman commander believing that a Jewish guy from the area is actually his "Lord"—capable of healing, performing miracles—and entrusting his eternal salvation to him. How is it possible to reconcile this with the rest of his life as a career military man, put in place to manage the Jewish resistance?

This soldier calling Jesus "Lord" was a major and possibly career and life-threatening breach of protocol. As a military man serving under Caesar, he pledged to worship him as his lord as though Caesar himself were a god. So if word got back to this man's commanding officer, he could be in big trouble, putting it lightly.

Leading up to this moment, this man had a history of caring for the Jews. Imbedded in the account is the recollection by his friends that this man built a synagogue for the Jewish people. His friends said he loved the Jews. We are not provided an explanation of why he loved the Jews but that he did built a house of worship for them. We only know that he didn't feel worthy of Jesus coming into his home. We also know that he believed it wasn't necessary for Jesus to complete the journey anyway. Stay there and say the word. My servant will be healed. "Yes sir!" would be the reply to that order by any abiding soldier.

Jesus' amazement at the faith of the Roman solder is his humanity in its fullness. God can't be amazed, right? The creator of all heaven and earth and all things in it can't be surprised. Check. The Lord Almighty is never astonished. Correct.

How else to be amazed

There is also another form of amazement that doesn't involve surprise. Perhaps Jesus in his humanity experienced this.

I once took a picture of the sunset with a hazy sky as it dropped below the trees at our lake cabin. I'm not a great photographer, but I must say, it turned out pretty good. I have kept this picture on my smartphone as the wallpaper, and when I see it, it takes me back to that place I enjoy so much.

Now I could show you my phone and that picture, and I'd expect you to say something like, "That's a pretty nice picture." And it is. However, if you had been standing shoulder to shoulder with me on that evening and had seen what I saw, you might say something more like, "That sunset is amazing!"

Even though you've seen many sunsets before this one, and you've even seen some pretty nice sunsets, let's face it, there are some that do look amazing. A picture, even a really good one, doesn't quite take the place of actually being there and experiencing it. So, there's no element of surprise involved. The amazement comes from being in the moment and experiencing something that is so beautiful, so un-common, that you just take it in. That's amazing.

We don't know the cause of Jesus' amazement, whether he was as-tonished or surprised, or that he found a certain beauty in the man's faith, knowing his background and vocation. In any case, Jesus in his humanity was amazed at this man's faith. I think nearly any other person in and around this story would have had the same reaction. Can you imagine the disciples and followers of Jesus being surprised that a Roman officer, one who has been charged specifically with op-pressing their movement, aligning with the same faith and belief they had? How about the Romans? Consider what the government officials or the other soldiers that witnessed this must have thought. Do you think this faith in a local Jew, son of a carpenter, would be amazing?

Although their reaction of surprise might be tempered with disap-pointment in him, I think it could be accurate to describe the Roman higher-ups' response to their officer's faith in the Jew from Nazareth to be one of surprise or amazement. So, it's not a stretch to imagine folks of the time period being amazed by the officer's faith. How about Jesus?

AMAZING THAT IT'S AMAZING

Jesus, in his humanity, could totally be surprised by this man's faith. Why wouldn't he? Everyone else proximate to the situation would likely be. Do you think it's amazing that this man could amaze Jesus? Is it reasonable to consider that everyone else —the disciples, Jesus' other followers, the Roman government, and the Roman soldiers— could have been amazed? Why not Jesus too?

Perhaps a bigger question is, "Can we still amaze Jesus?" Picture this. You've died and gone on to heaven. It's now time that you'll finally meet Jesus face-to-face, in all his glory. Wow! And what if he says to you, "*Fill in your name here*, remember that time when you helped that person and were really inconvenienced by that and how much money that cost you? Dude, that was amazing!"

Okay, so Jesus might not say "dude" to you, although, don't rule that out entirely. What would your reaction be? I think you could knock me over with a feather if Jesus would tell me that. Wow! Is this even possible?

We can rely on the example of scripture. It happened once. It's true. There actually lived a man that amazed Jesus. Isn't that wonderful? That someone could amaze Jesus? If it happened once, is it possible that it could be accomplished by another? I'd like to think so. I want to think so anyway. That I could amaze Jesus. That you could amaze Jesus. How did the soldier amaze Jesus?

HIS FAITH DID IT

Jesus was amazed by the soldier's faith. Jesus was amazed at a man who had such a strong faith in the face of possible expulsion from his career as a military man. Not only could his faith cost him his career but also his life. He had a faith that led him to love others and provide from his means to build a synagogue. Yet, while dedicated to his career, he cared for his servant enough to enlist the help of Jesus to heal him. Given these circumstances, this man had an amazing faith.

How about us?

How does my faith hold up under the pressure of challenging circumstances in various environments? How about at work, with family, and with friends? Am I ethical, fair, and honest in my decisions especially when it's difficult or unpopular? Do I have integrity and consistency in my character? Do I love others to the point of sacrificing for them? Have I decided to live on less so others can have more?

What kind of faith would amaze Jesus? Looking at the example of the Roman soldier, it was a faith that was pure . . . unwavering . . . thoughtful . . . risky . . . sacrificing . . . loving. I wonder if a demonstration of our faith that exhibits these characteristics might possibly amaze Jesus today.

How about we set out to have the kind of faith that might amaze Jesus?

STUDY QUESTIONS

1. When have you been in charge of others and provided direction or instructions? When your authority was respected and followed, what was the end result?

2. Why did the Roman soldier ask Jesus to come to his house? What did he seem to believe about Jesus?

3. List some things in nature that amaze you.

4. Describe how you might feel if you heard Jesus describe your faith as amazing.

5. What has God done in your life that you would describe as amazing?

amazed

JESUS
WEPT

Jesus wept.   John 11:35 NIV

The shortest verse in the Bible. As a kid growing up, I remember in Sunday school we were sometimes urged to memorize scripture. My response, while under the pressure of achievement, was always "I've got one, 'Jesus wept,'" then follow that with my laughter due to my own sense of cleverness. However, I did not know the name of the book, chapter, or verse of the Bible in which this brief passage appears. I hope I'm not the only child that attempted to get away with this.

The background for the two recorded circumstances in which we find Jesus weeping is quite interesting.

SICK FRIEND

Jesus was hanging out in Jerusalem doing what he did best—performing miracles of healing and teaching, and challenging the religious folks of the day. Just down the road a few miles in Bethany, his friend

Lazarus was sick and near death. His sisters, Mary and Martha, were also well-known to Jesus. The sisters sent a message to Jesus that his pal was very sick. Jesus loved this family, but rather than hustling along to check on his friend, he hung out in Jerusalem for a couple more days before making the short trip to Bethany. The reason he waited to leave for Bethany isn't stated. All we know is that Jesus didn't leave right away upon getting the notice of his friend's condition. Then things started to get interesting.

WHY DIDN'T YOU COME SOONER?

Jesus arrived in Bethany and was told Lazarus had died four days earlier. When Martha was told Jesus was in town, she went to see him. To me, she seemed a little put off that Jesus didn't come right away to heal her brother. She second-guessed Jesus on why he didn't come sooner.

> Martha said to Jesus, "Lord, if only you had been here, my brother would not have died." John 11:21

Martha might have been upset with Jesus, but she also knew he could still affect the situation. Naturally she was upset about her brother having recently died. But she did call on Jesus and the power he had to plead with him to perform a miracle.

> "But even now I know that God will give you whatever you ask." John 11:22

Jesus, as he was so masterful at doing, turned this into a teachable moment for Martha. He affirmed to her that her brother would rise again. Martha mistook this to be at the resurrection of Jesus' followers, which would include her brother, sometime in the undefined future. Jesus took the opportunity to state something about himself—something that has been repeated throughout the centuries. Jesus told Martha that he himself is life, and that belief in him means eternal life. Jesus then asked for Martha's affirmation of this. "Do you believe this, Martha?" Jesus asked. "Yes, Lord," was her reply. It's simply wonderful how Jesus turned sorrow, anger, and accusation into hope for the future. A future with him.

> *Jesus told her, "I am the resurrection and the life. Anyone who believes in me will live, even after dying. Everyone who lives in me and believes in me will never die."* John 11:25–26a

TAKE TWO

Next comes Mary. Similar situation. Mary pulled the old "should of, could of, would of" thing on Jesus. Mary said, "Lord, if only you had been here, my brother would not have died" (John 11:32). Mary then wept in his presence. There were others there, too, present for this conversation. They also cried. Verse 33 says a deep anger welled up in Jesus, and he was deeply troubled. Another translation says Jesus "groaned in the spirit and was troubled" (NKJV). Jesus asked, "Where have you put him?" "Lord, come and see," he was told (John 11:34). Then, it happened.

Jesus wept.

TEARY WATCHING TELEVISION

Did this scene about Lazarus strike you as strange? Think about it. Jesus as God knew the power available to him from the Father, having displayed it on several occasions. Scripture records that Jesus had already performed several other miracles, including raising another from the dead (the widow's son from Nain) not to mention turning water into wine, and healing people. So Jesus knew what was possible. And Jesus as God would even know what was going to happen. So why get so weepy?

Have you ever watched a movie and were moved to tears? Come on guys, admit it. Even if you choked back the water works and didn't actually cry, you did feel the emotions well up inside. Why would that be? Even stranger, have you ever watched a movie of a true story with a happy ending that stirred you emotionally—and even though you knew how it was going to end, you still felt emotional?

I recall watching *The Bible* series created by Mark Burnett and Roma Downey. There were many opportunities to become emotional during this show. But most pale in comparison to the torture and crucifixion scenes of Jesus. Little was held back. The brutalizing, beating, humiliating, and ultimate cross-hanging death was shown in a very realistic fashion. These scenes moved me to tears. As I watched, I thought of how this must have felt. I thought of how unjust his punishment was. I thought of how he did this for us. He didn't have to, but he chose to. Words can do little to describe this sacrifice.

And yet, I knew the ending. I knew Jesus' physical suffering would end. I knew he would be raised from the dead. I knew he would come back to hang out with his friends and followers for about six weeks. And I knew he would return home to be with the Father. I knew all this and still cried as I watched.

I also knew it wasn't real. It was a movie. An actor was playing Jesus. The situations were staged. Jesus wasn't really harmed in any way, nevertheless murdered by hanging on a cross. I knew what I was watching wasn't what it appeared to be. To put it bluntly, it was faked.

My feelings were those of empathy. I was identifying with Jesus, portrayed by an actor, as I watched on my television. Vicariously, I was living through what it might have been like to be him in that moment. I also wept at the injustice of the proceedings. Earlier in the movie, Jesus was depicted as kind, gentle, and loving. So it seemed really unfair to see him treated in this way. I also felt a deep sense of gratitude. Thankful for what he did for me. Some combination of, or the sum of, these feelings stirred me to the point of weeping. Weeping just as Jesus wept.

PART OF THE SADNESS

So Jesus' friend was dead. Jesus knew his friend suffered from some unnamed sickness before he died. Maybe it was painful. Maybe his death wasn't peaceful. The sisters, Martha and Mary, were close friends of Jesus. He knew them. He saw the pain in their faces. He might have noticed red eyes from days of crying tears. He sensed the desperation in their questioning of him. Then, as Jesus approached Lazarus's tomb, he encountered the mourners. It seems to me Lazarus might have been well loved. One version describes the mourners at the tomb to be "wailing." That's crying with an explanation point.

It all came crashing down on Jesus. A sick friend suffering death. Loving sisters missing their brother. And all the others, so many people, all missing this one man. It was an emotionally charged moment. I can only think the appropriate response for Jesus to have was to join the others in their sorrow. So Jesus wept.

A DONKEY, A PARADE, AND TEARS

There is a second occasion recorded in the gospels when Jesus wept. It's recorded in Luke 13. Jesus was making his triumphal entry into the city of Jerusalem, the home base for his people. He mounted a small donkey, and as he rode it, the people in the crowds put their coats on the road ahead of him. A first-century version of the red carpet treatment we see used for modern-day dignitaries. The crowds were shouting and singing praises for the miracles they witnessed.

As he approached the city, Jesus began to cry. Jesus was expressing his regret that the people of Jerusalem had not found the "way of peace" and that it was too late for them to do so. He was sorrowful that the city and the people in it would be destroyed by its enemies.

> But as he came closer to Jerusalem and saw the city ahead, he began to weep. "How I wish today that you of all people would understand the way of peace. But now it is too late, and peace is hidden from your eyes. Before long your enemies will build ramparts against your walls and encircle you and close in on you from every side." Luke 19:41–43

Jesus knew what the others didn't know. He knew that in 70 CE the city and its more than one million people[1] would perish in a gruesome display of terror and destruction. Beyond that, he knew the coming future of the Jewish people: the twentieth-century holocaust and the embattlements carried out in the city into our present day. Are these some of the reasons that caused him to weep?

Jesus came to save the lost. He might have had a heightened sense of grief for the people of Jerusalem in that they missed the opportunity to be saved, especially as he appeared on earth as a man at that time. What simpler time to find faith in him than when he appeared to them in the flesh? Performed many miracles for them to see. Spent time in their synagogues teaching from scripture and pointing out so clearly how he fulfilled what he has read. And now those same people were about to torture and hang him on a cross to die in a matter of a few days.

Jesus might have been grieving over all of this. His people. His city. Lost opportunity. Their chance to be saved. Knowing the outcome for those who would be lost. He was not willing that anyone should perish. All of this, the destruction of the city in the coming decades, the abuse and murdering of the Jews in the prison camps during World War II, and perhaps the wider rejection that all humanity made of Jesus as our savior.

Pastor Greg Laurie wrote this in his blog on Jesus.

> Why did Jesus weep when He saw Jerusalem? Being God and having omniscience, Jesus knew these fickle people who were crying out, "Hosanna!" would soon be shouting, "Crucify Him!" He knew that one of His handpicked disciples, Judas, would betray Him. He knew that another disciple, Peter, would deny Him. He knew that Caiaphas, the high priest, would conspire with Pilate, the Roman governor, to bring about His death. And, He knew the future of Jerusalem. Looking ahead 40 years, He saw the destruction that would come upon the city at the hands of the Emperor Titus and his Roman legions.
>
> Jesus also wept because His ministry was almost over. Time was short. He had healed their sick. He had raised their dead. He had cleansed their lepers. He had fed their hungry. He

had forgiven their sins. Yet for the most part, He had been rejected.[2]

It is difficult to imagine the death of a child. When we hear of such a loss, we are all saddened. It seems so tragic, so wrong, so unfair. It's hard to hear about this on the news and not be affected.

How about the loss of one of your own children? I haven't experienced this, but I know people who have. It is certainly sad and tragic having this happen to someone else. Some of you reading this now have actually experienced this. My heart cries out for you. I am failing to find words to express my feelings. The truth is I have no idea how you must feel. You have my deepest sympathy.

Jesus might have felt like this. These were his own people. His children. And he knew their future, their destiny. And it was not good, and actually it was tragic on eternal proportions. So Jesus wept.

How does it feel to know that our God has cried? That he felt empathy? Jesus seemed to show empathy in these moments when he cried as well as in the many other times he performed healing miracles. Most commentaries on Jesus' possible motives for healing indicate they were not as much to demonstrate God's power, although they certainly do. Another reason is that Jesus might have been compelled to perform physical healing on several people he encountered during his three-year ministry was because he wanted to restore the afflicted out of his compassion for them.

Scripture reveals Jesus' compassion and empathy for us, too. And God through Jesus has felt sorrow, pain, and loss. He knows what it's like to lose a loved one. To mourn. To be in sorrow. He knows. He's felt it. Just as we have.

Rest assured that as we move through this life, it is only certain that we will feel pain. We will experience loss. We will be sorrowful. We will mourn. We will suffer. So has Jesus. He's been in your place. He has shown his empathy for others. And he has this same empathy for you when you suffer now. Right now today. For you.

STUDY QUESTIONS

1. Why do you think Jesus wept over his friend Lazarus's death?

2. When watching a TV program or movie or reading a book, why is it possible that we become emotional? How about even when we know the ending?

3. Why did Jesus weep over Jerusalem?

4. Why do you think it was important for Jesus to display this very human emotion?

5. Are you more, less, or equally likely to become emotional over a personal loss of your own or over a loss of someone else's? Why might that be?

amazed

JESUS
WAS ANGRY

Jesus entered the Temple and began to drive out all the people buying and selling animals for sacrifice. He knocked over the tables of the money changers and the chairs of those selling doves. He said to them, "The Scriptures declare, 'My Temple will be called a house of prayer,' but you have turned it into a den of thieves!" Matthew 21:12–13

Okay, let's start with an admission. Nowhere in the verses above does it actually say that Jesus was angry. But would you agree that his words and actions appear like the actions of an angry man? In this chapter we'll look at some times when Jesus displayed his anger. First, there's a big question associated with this discussion.

Is it a sin to have anger?

That is a really important question.

Although anger is absolutely a human emotion, it isn't exclusively human. Not only was Jesus in his humanity angry, God the Father also demonstrated anger as documented many times in the Old Testament. Frequently the Father's anger is characterized as "wrath." Wrath is defined as "strong vengeful anger or indignation" by Merriam-Webster's dictionary.[1]

Furthermore, the word *indignation*, nestled within the previous definition, further sheds light on God's feelings. Indignation is defined as "anger caused by something that is unfair or wrong."[2] So when we witness something unjust or simply just plain mean being done to someone, that makes us mad.

WRATH POURED OUT IN OLD TESTAMENT TIMES

Before Pharaoh allowed the Israelites to leave Egypt, God sent a final plague over the land. It was so severe and so personal to Pharaoh that he finally relented and set the Israelite slaves free.

> *And that night at midnight, the Lord struck down all the firstborn sons in the land of Egypt, from the firstborn son of Pharaoh, who sat on his throne, to the firstborn son of the prisoner in the dungeon. Even the firstborn of their livestock were killed. Pharaoh and all his officials and all the people of Egypt woke up during the night, and loud wailing was heard throughout the land of Egypt. There was not a single house where someone had not died.*
> Exodus 12:29–30

This must have been a terrifying night for all who were there. We can only imagine. What led up to this was more than four hundred years of oppressing the Israelites in slavery by Pharaoh and his predecessors. Nine other plagues and verbal warnings were delivered from Moses and Aaron on God's behalf along with the request to let their people go. Then finally, God's mighty hand intervened on the behalf of the tormented.

God the Father showed his indignation in the Garden of Eden, too.

> *The serpent was the shrewdest of all the wild animals the Lord*
> *God had made. One day he asked the woman, "Did God really*
> *say you must not eat the fruit from any of the trees in the gar-*
> *den?" "Of course we may eat fruit from the trees in the garden,"*
> *the woman replied. "It's only the fruit from the tree in the middle*
> *of the garden that we are not allowed to eat. God said, 'You must*
> *not eat it or even touch it; if you do, you will die.'" "You won't die!"*
> *the serpent replied to the woman. "God knows that your eyes will*
> *be opened as soon as you eat it, and you will be like God, knowing*
> *both good and evil." The woman was convinced. She saw that the*
> *tree was beautiful and its fruit looked delicious, and she wanted*
> *the wisdom it would give her. So she took some of the fruit and ate*
> *it. Then she gave some to her husband, who was with her, and he*
> *ate it, too.* Genesis 3:1-6

Once God discovered their sin, he expelled them (and therefore us) from paradise on earth until he restores it to his glory in the future. Not only that, he issued several other curses that include pain in childbirth, hard work to survive in this world, and physical death, all of which were not included in God's original blueprint for our lives.

Look back a few verses and you'll find God's direction and warning.

> *But the Lord God warned him, "You may freely eat the fruit of*
> *every tree in the garden—except the tree of the knowledge of good*
> *and evil. If you eat its fruit, you are sure to die."* Genesis 2:16-17

So God, who was originally walking through the garden and spending time with Adam and Eve, now discharged them from his physical presence. God cannot be in the presence of sin. And Adam and Eve when falling to the serpent's temptation, brought sin into the garden and therefore into the world.

There are many other examples in the Old Testament of God's wrath or indignation. For brevity sake, I selected only two, which are familiar to many. Two is a small sample size upon which to build a conclusion so I encourage you to do your own research. An Internet search of "God's anger" will show many references.

ARE THERE ANY OTHER OPTIONS?

God provides instruction, direction, or a way out before he brings his wrath. God is big on justice, and he epitomizes this through his actions.

The Egyptians had 430 years to get it right. Then Pharaoh was warned by Moses and Aaron. And after nine plagues, a patient God brought his wrath with a tenth and final plague.

God instructed and gave Adam full charge of his garden, even letting him name all the animals. God told Adam there was only one thing to stay away from—the tree of the knowledge of good and evil. Even though Adam had the run of the place and the knowledge of what not to do, he and Eve caved in to temptation. Then God removed them from the garden.

One thing we can take from observing God's wrath as recorded in scripture is that it demonstrates to us the permanent consequence of living apart from him. But this condition need not be permanent. God's desire is to be with us and for us to be with him. Even though we are separated from God by sin, we can choose to ask God to let us enter his kingdom, and he has promised to allow us in.

Reading the accounts of the Old Testament shows the shortsightedness and arrogance of the human race. Time and time again God showed up, extended mercy, provided for the people's needs, and bailed them out of trouble, but in short order God was cast out and forgotten. Before you are too quick to harshly judge those you read about in the Old Testament, think how alike their rebellion in response to a loving God is similar to ours in the present day. Perhaps not that much has changed.

So Jesus, the God-man, became angry too. There is more than one instance recorded when Jesus either demonstrated or explicitly noted his anger.

TEMPER IN THE TEMPLE AND ON THE SABBATH

In his final trip back to Jerusalem, Jesus went into the temple. This was his Father's house, a place of worship. People traveled long distances in pilgrimage to visit and worship God, offering their best sacrifices, as was the custom of the time. Many came from foreign lands and long distances, too far to carry much more than what was required for the trip.

Upon arriving at the temple, people exchanged their money and maybe purchased an animal to use for their sacrifice. This was a captive audience. Kind of like going to the airport, passing through the lengthy security lines, then becoming hungry, knowing that the restaurants can charge almost anything. If you're hungry, you'll pay. The money changers were taking advantage of the people desiring to worship.

When they arrived back in Jerusalem, Jesus entered the Temple and began to drive out the people buying and selling animals for sacrifices. He knocked over the tables of the money changers and the chairs of those selling doves, and he stopped everyone from using the Temple as a marketplace. He said to them, "The Scriptures declare, 'My Temple will be called a house of prayer for all nations,' but you have turned it into a den of thieves."
Mark 11:15–17

Earlier in his ministry, Jesus arrived at the synagogue on the Sabbath, the day of worship and rest. He noticed there was a man with a deformed hand. The religious leaders, defined as Jesus' "enemies" in some translations, were watching closely. Was Jesus going to heal the man's hand and violate the rule of resting on Sabbath?

Jesus said to the man with the deformed hand, "Come and stand in front of everyone." Then he turned to his critics and asked, "Does the law permit good deeds on the Sabbath, or is it a day for doing evil? Is this a day to save life or to destroy it?" But they wouldn't answer him. He looked around at them angrily and was deeply saddened by their hard hearts. Then he said to the man,

81

"Hold out your hand." So the man held out his hand, and it was restored! At once the Pharisees went away and met with the supporters of Herod to plot how to kill Jesus. Mark 3:3-6

Jesus was angry. He was angry about how people missed the point. He was upset with their lack of compassion. The Pharisees could have shown compassion or celebrated that this man who was once suffering with this physical abnormality was now fully restored! How wonderful! Let's rejoice! No, said the Pharisees, let's lament the fact that the rules were violated. Things are out of balance. This just isn't right. They seemed not to consider the purpose of the rules. Whose rules were these anyway? What were the rules to protect us from? There appears to be no grace from these guys.

Was Jesus' anger in these situations justified? If so, is the anger I feel from time to time also?

Remember the earlier discussion on indignation, defined as "anger aroused by something unjust, unworthy, or mean"? Jesus was indignant in these circumstances. In both cases, people were being victimized—the money changers taking unfair financial advantage of those desiring to worship God and the man with the deformed hand would not have been healed if the Pharisees had their way. Jesus sensed the injustice, unfairness, victimization, and the cruelty being waged on these people. Clearly, justified anger.

OUR COMMON ANGER

What about our anger and when might it be justified?

For example, I'm driving home from work and coming to an intersection with a signal light. There is a long line of cars coming from my right waiting to use the intersection. I have a green light, so naturally theirs is red. A vehicle in the right-turn lane, having a red light, turns right and comes into my lane, causing me to slow down significantly. No crash, but a big inconvenience. I can't move to my left due to others cars trapping me in my lane. I'm in a hurry to get home. Finally

I can pull into the left-hand lane and I buzz by the car that violated my personal space. I look right and notice the driver, the one who cut me off, is deep in conversation on a mobile phone and didn't even notice my angry glance toward him. (I stopped the response at "angry glance," but let's be honest here, there are other responses to this, none of which we're proud of!)

Justified anger? Was there a real injustice, actual harm, or violation of rights occurring here? No, it was just another hassle in life.

When I'm honest and examine many of the situations that make me angry, I must put them in the selfish category. I'm not proud of that. Too many times I get angry about things that aren't on my original agenda, not my plan, people disrespecting me, hassling me, putting me at risk, being inconsiderate, and the list goes on. As I take inventory of those situations, truth is that I'm making it about me and not about others. I'm stuck on myself and less concerned about the actual welfare of others. Not always, but many of the times when I feel anger and it's about someone's effect on me, it has been selfish.

Do we have the capacity to have indignation or righteous anger? I believe we do.

I was serving breakfast at one of our local homeless shelters early one morning. An ambulance showed up and the EMTs were in the process of bringing someone out on a stretcher. The female patient was conscious and seemed alert so I assumed the situation wasn't serious, but apparently she was in need of medical treatment. I made a passing comment to one of the EMTs just as they were about to drive off, "It sure would be nice if there were another option for medical care than the need to call you guys." The EMT I was addressing turned to me and said, "I'm not sure that would matter with these people."

"These people." Really? Who exactly are these people? I felt my ire rise just a bit. I felt I was a just witness to a moment of judgment reigning down on this woman whom I imagined was desperate, in need of medical care, and having no other options available to her. Perhaps I was misjudging the context in which the EMT meant his comment to be taken. I guess I'm not really sure. I just know that I felt like someone needed to stick up for this woman. She didn't ask to be in this situation. I'll bet she'd rather not have been on that stretcher and living at a homeless shelter.

Was the anger I felt justified? I'll leave that up to you.

ANGER—SIN OR NOT SIN?

So is it sin to have anger? If God the Father showed his anger and Jesus did as well, it seems that anger itself is not a sin.

Anger can be used to tempt us into sin similar to how lust does. My *response* to that is what's critical. After the first glance, I have a choice to make. Look again? And again? Capture that thought in my mind? Remember it for later? Tell my buddies about it? Make a comment? Or take no other glance, maybe move from the physical surroundings if possible, and turn my thoughts to something else. Sin or not sin. My choice of response determines this.

I am responsible for my response to my feelings of anger. When I was cut off by the driver in the earlier story, I could have remained a comfortable distance behind and not passed him. Or even better, I could have passed him, smiled, and waved a little wave to let him know I wasn't upset. The response is up to me.

God's anger toward sin and means of dealing with it is a central part of the story of the cross. Jesus' purpose is to make a way for us to the Father. We can't be in relationship with the Father because of our sinful nature. God can't be a part of that. Just as he separated himself from Adam and Eve in the garden, we are separate from him without the cross.

Here's a big word—propitiation. This involves appeasing or satisfying the wrath of the Father and being reconciled to him. There's that word *wrath* again.

We have no way to satisfy God's wrath over the sin in this world. We can't be good enough and can't do enough. No matter what we do or try, we always screw up again at some point. We've all chosen the selfish over the selfless and hurt others in the process. It's just too difficult to get it right, all the time, every time.

That's where Jesus comes in. He did get it right. He led a sinless life. God made a way for us to be reconciled to himself. It's through Jesus.

> *For all have sinned and fall short of the glory of God, being justified freely by His grace through the redemption that is in Christ Jesus, whom God set forth as a propitiation by His blood, through faith, to demonstrate His righteousness, because in His forbearance God had passed over the sins that were previously committed.*
> Romans 3:23–25 NKJV

God the Father has shown his anger. It's recorded during Jesus' time on Earth as a man, that he also showed his anger. The anger was justified as it was over sin. And God poured out his anger over sin at the cross, and Jesus bore that for us so we don't have to. We only need to choose him.

And our anger? Sure, we feel it. It's natural and normal to feel anger. What we get angry about and our response to our feelings of anger matter to God. So, let's allow it to matter to us.

STUDY QUESTIONS

1. What are some of the times that God has become angry?

2. What kind of things cause you to be angry?

3. Explain justified anger. Who is being wronged in most of these instances?

4. What was the source of anger Jesus had when turning over the tables in the temple?

5. Explain "propitiation" in your own words.

CHAPTER NINE

JESUS
SERVED

For even the Son of Man came not to be served but to serve others and to give his life as a ransom for many." **Matthew 20:28**

Jesus has a way of turning everything upside down. Jesus has a new world order that is in stark contrast to what we might have learned, seen, observed, or taught. Jesus as God and man, author and creator of all things seen and unseen, also identifies himself as a servant.

This chapter will examine three principal ways in which Jesus served. As a matter of fact, he told us that one of his purposes was to come into the world to set an example for us of being a servant.

Jesus' disciples were among the Jews waiting on a new king and kingdom. This was a much-prophesied and long-foretold truth that was known and expected by the Jews of Jesus' day. Dozens of verses in the Old Testament point to Jesus. Examples range from where and to whom he would be born and the identity of his family lineage right down to how he would be tortured, die a physical death, and rise again.

> *"All right then, the Lord himself will give you the sign. Look! The virgin will conceive a child! She will give birth to a son and will call him Immanuel (which means 'God is with us')."* Isaiah 7:14

A KINGDOM HARD TO IMAGINE

More than a dozen times it's recorded that Jesus taught on the kingdom of heaven and kingdom of God. The Jews asked for and got earthly kings several times during their people's history. It had been hundreds of years since the Jews had their own king. In Jesus' time, they were under Roman rule without a king of their own. One could certainly see how early expectations for Jesus as a leader would be high.

Jesus was talking about kingdoms. Performing miracles. Teaching with a deep wisdom. And fulfilling scripture as he lived his life.

Matthew 20:28 opened this chapter. The scene before that passage was when the mother of two of the disciples, James and John, asked Jesus to create a special place in his kingdom for her sons. She seems like a real first century "helicopter mom" hovering over her sons' future. More conversation ensued that was overheard by the other disciples. Boy, did they get upset. There's twelve of these guys—eating, sleeping, walking, talking, working, and struggling day after day with Jesus as he traveled and taught. Then two of the guys' mom tried to angle in on a way for her boys to get special treatment. Yeah, I think I get why they were upset.

Just then, Jesus turned the conversation into a lesson on the contrast between the kingdom he is speaking of and the one they are currently subject to.

> *But Jesus called them together and said, "You know that the rulers in this world lord it over their people, and officials flaunt their authority over those under them. But among you it will be*

different. Whoever wants to be a leader among you must be your servant, and whoever wants to be first among you must become your slave." Matthew 20:25-27

I wonder if this was a puzzling statement for the disciples (and the mother of James and John) to comprehend. We all know that servants are lowly. That's why Zebedee's wife asked for better for her two sons, James and John. What mother wouldn't?

The disciples had a front-row seat to the life of Jesus, the original servant leader. Before their time together on earth ended, they experienced Jesus performing many miracles of physical healing. He washed their feet and then sacrificed himself on the cross for their, and our, benefit. First, consider the healing miracles Jesus performed.

HEALING MIRACLES SHOW JESUS' COMPASSION

In his book *Jesus before Christianity,* Albert Nolan makes this observation: "Anyone who thinks that Jesus' motive for performing miracles of healing was a desire to prove something, to prove that he was the Messiah or Son of God, has thoroughly misunderstood him. His one and only motive for healing people was compassion."[1]

Phillip Yancy, in his book *The Jesus I Never Knew,* says, "Jesus asked us his followers to do three things to remember him. He asked us to baptize others, just as he had been baptized by John. He asked us to remember the meal he shared that very evening with the disciples. Finally, he asked us to wash one another's feet."[2]

The meal referred to is understood to be what we now call communion. That regular event in the church centers us, provides a means for forgiveness, and causes us to recall the sacrifice Jesus made for us in his submission to death on the cross.

Yancy goes on to quote the famous American theologian, Jonathan Edwards, in that "God has designated the poor as his 'receivers.'"[3] We can't do anything for God, as he is fully self-sufficient as well as the maker and creator of all things. So God has delegated the task of receiving the giver's gifts to those in need.

I was at a conference a few years ago where a speaker was telling a story about a time when he was responsible for the "handling" of Mother Teresa. He was part of the team to get her to an appointment to speak at a certain time as well as to her next engagement. The speaker marveled at how the agenda didn't matter to her. She saw someone in need along the side of the road, so she directed the driver to pull over so she could get out of the car and come to the person's aid. Mother Teresa had only one agenda—to serve God and others. Nothing else mattered.

I have pictured Jesus like this—stopping off from the planned travels to heal someone and relieve that person from an ailment. He was always willing step into a situation in which he could help. I wonder how the disciples took this. Peter seemed to be what we would now call a "type A" personality. A real go-getter. Do you think he would sigh when they'd stop off to help someone or maybe blurt out, "Hey, Jesus, you've got a teaching engagement at the temple in an hour. We better get going!" Of course this isn't recorded as happening, but I do think Jesus showed his followers what really mattered. And to Jesus, showing compassion to those in need mattered a great deal more than any earthly agenda.

It might depend on your research source, but I've read there were thirty-seven miracles performed by Jesus that were recorded. This doesn't include the ones mentioned at the end of the gospel of John that weren't written down. Many of the miracles performed by Jesus, more than three-quarters by my count, met the urgent physical needs of people—whether it be feeding or healing them. Jesus seemed to exhibit a great deal of compassion for the suffering of people in his time.

JESUS THE FOOT WASHER

So why would Jesus wash the disciples feet?

Feet are used to carry one from place to place when walking. Feet perspire, providing the perfect host for fungi. During Jesus' day, most footwear, if any were worn at all, were open. Think of a sandal. This might have helped a bit with the fungus issue, but walking along the dusty roads that included dodging animal manure all day long would result in very dirty feet.

The custom for a communal meal at the time was to recline, perhaps leaning on one side or the other, next to a rather low table. If you've seen a depiction of the Last Supper with all the disciples sitting on one side of the table with Jesus in the center, well, it's unlikely to have happened that way. It's more likely they were crowded around a low table, lying a bit sideways or reclining. So in this posture, one's feet could likely end up near another diner's face. Pretty gross.

In the case of a group meal, the host would instruct the servants to care for the guests, which included bringing in the food, refilling drinks, and at the start of things, washing the patrons' feet.

One of the ministries in which I serve provides a daily breakfast to more than one hundred homeless people in Minneapolis. Yes, daily. We provide the food, prepare it, set up the service tables, serve the meal, and tear down and wash the service items all in the span of about two and one-half hours. Daily. I'm so inspired when I see the dedication of the folks on these seven teams (one for each day of the week) arrive at 4:30 a.m. to start things in motion. I love this ministry.

One of the customs is that annually on Good Friday we offer to wash the feet of our meal guests. People are very tentative to allow us to do this, but every year we get a handful of takers. If you've never done this before, I recommend it. It is a most humbling experience to wash another's feet. We first bathe them in a warm bath with Epson salts, dry them carefully, rub on lotion, and then put on a fresh, new clean pair of socks.

The truth is, in my humanity, it's pretty gross. It's awkward to ask someone to allow me to do this. And when someone agrees, it is a little clumsy to get started. The feet I've had the honor of washing have been pretty disgusting. I once actually watched a guy pull off a toenail right in front of me! Yikes!

You can imagine that even among the servants, this job was not reserved for the head of the staff. I wonder if it was left for the lowest servant of all. This is the role Jesus elected to step into. The lowest job of all.

Peter, of course, was the one who pushed back at Jesus offering to wash his feet.

> *When Jesus came to Simon Peter, Peter said to him, "Lord, are you going to wash my feet?"* John 13:6

Jesus told Peter that he wouldn't understand now but would later. After Peter's continued protest, Jesus finally told him that if he didn't wash him, he wouldn't belong to him (Jesus). Not only was this a hygiene issue for the meal, but Jesus was using this as a symbolic teaching moment. Jesus seemed never to miss the opportunity to turn every situation into something greater. There is a great lesson to be learned here. I can't state it better than Jesus did. Here is his capstone comment on the reason for washing their feet.

> *"And since I, your Lord and Teacher, have washed your feet, you ought to wash each other's feet. I have given you an example to follow. Do as I have done to you."* John 13:14–15

And there's the lesson. We look into the life of Jesus—how he conducted himself during his time on earth, how he treated others—and we emulate him. By my count, it is recorded eleven times in the gospels that Jesus said, "Follow me." That means do as I do and have a heart like mine. So that's it, follow me. Big lesson.

THE GREATEST GIFT OF A SERVANT-LEADER

The final way in which Jesus served is his sacrifice on the cross. This is a huge topic that can and has filled complete books. My comments only scratch the surface and relate to how Jesus served in his humanity.

Jesus served us by his sacrifice. I love the words of the apostle Paul in Philippians, which say it all.

Though he was God, he did not think of equality with God as something to cling to. Instead, he gave up his divine privileges; he took the humble position of a slave and was born as a human being. When he appeared in human form, he humbled himself in obedience to God and died a criminal's death on a cross.
Philippians 2:6–8

Does this not sound strikingly familiar to how Jesus handled the whole foot-washing situation? Jesus' character is consistent through and through, in every situation and with everyone.

Jesus did what he didn't have to do. Jesus is God. Yet he gave up his rightful place on his throne along with all that goes with that: honor, glory, worship. Instead he became one of us, joined our ranks. He did it without making a big deal about it.

Every year near Christmas time, the Salvation Army rolls out its well-known red kettle campaign. Red kettles collect donations outside popular shopping establishments while volunteers ring bells near the kettle to capture people's attention.

A couple of years ago in my community, the campaign was in serious trouble. Christmas was fast approaching and the fund drive wasn't anywhere near the set target. Then out of nowhere came an anonymous donor (or donors, no one knows) who dropped large donations amounting to tens of thousands of dollars in kettles at a variety of locations around the city. When I searched the Internet to find this exact story, to my surprise this wasn't unique. My search turned up dozens of stories of mystery givers leaving large amounts of cash, gold coins, jewelry, and even gold bars in the red kettles! In each case the giver chose not to be identified. They weren't seeking glory or recognition, but simply elected to give.

Think about Jesus' earthly ministry. Think about how you or I might have gone about it, knowing full well we have all the resources in the universe at our disposal. I might have first dethroned all the earthly leaders and taken over. Disbanded all the armies, set up aid sites for those in need, and built many places to worship so it would be convenient to everyone to make it to church. Only the best and the brightest would be chosen for the task. Then I might have publicly held hearings for those who were oppressing others and rendered justice on the perpetrators. I guess in my impatience, I would have wanted to bring God's kingdom to earth right then. But God wants to give all the opportunity to come to him. He is not only loving, but also patient.

Instead, Jesus selected a few people, men and women willing to follow him. For the most part, they were ordinary, little-educated, working-class people. For the short span of three years, he traveled in the region, never venturing far from his hometown, teaching in synagogues, on hillsides, at beaches, and anywhere else he could get an audience. He never held political office and had no distribution channels of his teachings organized during his lifetime. And even though the miracles he performed were truly just that, miraculous, only a handful of people experienced the benefit of these, and a limited number of people witnessed this firsthand. Jesus didn't make a big deal about himself or his ministry.

Instead he made himself nothing. Took the humble position of a slave. Became a man. Even more, he chose to die the death reserved only for the most despicable criminals. To be tortured, beaten, and hung on a cross. The most terrible form of punishment and death that could be imagined. That's humility and service.

There was a new homeless shelter built in the Twin Cities a few years ago. Nice place. New construction. Everything was fresh and clean unlike most shelters I've been in. Only one thing was missing. I figured it out pretty quickly during one of my first visits. Nothing was offered to help people deal with the brokenness of homelessness—the loss of dignity, hopelessness, and separation of all things good—that is commonly felt among this population. Driving home from one of my early visits, my heart was broken and I was crying. I couldn't stop. I felt like someone must bring hope to these folks. Jesus is the source of my hope, and my sorrow was over the fact that no one was bringing Jesus into that shelter.

Then it hit me. If I recognize the problem, I own the problem. It's not really "my problem." I didn't put these folks on the street. I didn't determine not to have any faith-based programming at this shelter. But I did recognize the problem. So, it's now my problem. I decided to start a Bible study and after a long process was turned down. Since then, I show up there once or twice per week bringing in articles that are needed for the residents—personal care stuff mostly along with reading materials—and spend time in the shelter area connecting with guys, talking, and often praying about their needs and hopes. It's not as tidy a program as I would like, but I recognize that my part is to be faithful and to show up when recognizing the problem. And I'm sure God has plans beyond this present state anyway. And I hope to be there when he does what he does.

Jesus personified this. This broken world wasn't his mess, wasn't his design, and wasn't his fault, but he stepped in and will see it through until it is finished.

Jesus served. He was compassionate and took time to provide physical and spiritual healing to several people during his earthly ministry. He humbled himself and set the best example of servant leadership by washing the disciples' feet during their last meal together on earth. And he made the ultimate sacrifice shortly thereafter by his torturous death so that we might be given a way into his kingdom and have everlasting life.

Jesus, his life on earth and his character, can be described in many ways. If he were to select only one word to describe himself, I wonder how likely it is Jesus would choose the term "servant." I think the odds on that one are pretty good.

STUDY QUESTIONS

1. What kind of kingdom did some of Jesus' followers mistakenly think he was going to set up?

2. How would you describe the paradox (opposite of what one might think) of leadership and servanthood?

3. Why do you think Jesus washed his disciples' feet?

4. How is it that we go about setting up our earthly kingdoms—nations, companies, organizations—that differ from what Jesus did?

5. Why do you think it was so important for Jesus to be a servant?

amazed

JESUS
PRAYED

After sending them home, he went up into the hills by himself to pray. Night fell while he was there alone. Matthew 14:23

The accounts of Jesus' life in the gospels of the Bible (Matthew, Mark, Luke, and John) tell that Jesus prayed a lot. I mean a lot. He prayed alone and in the presence of others. He often thanked God, and he also asked for things of God. He prayed sorrowful prayers. He prayed for others. Jesus prayed often.

It may sound surprising, but Jesus didn't always get the answer to his prayer as he asked it. Does that happen to you? I bet it does. It happens to me, too. Not having my agenda met in the way or timing of my request.

Did you know Jesus also prayed for you? Yup, really, he did. Roughly two thousand years ago, Jesus thought about you and me and prayed to the Father for us and about us. I think that is amazing. I think that is real love.

GOES WAY, WAY BACK

Prayer has been a staple for believers in God since the beginning of recorded scripture. If you look back in chapters one and two of Genesis, the first book in the Bible, God created everything, including humankind. In chapter three, Adam and Eve decided to do things their own way and stained the world with sin. By chapter four of Genesis, people were reaching out to God in worship.

> *When Seth grew up, he had a son and named him Enosh. At that time people first began to worship the Lord by name.* Genesis 4:26

> *Hear my prayer, O Lord! Listen to my cries for help! Don't ignore my tears. For I am your guest—a traveler passing through as my ancestors were before me.* Psalm 39:12

David is the boy who slayed the giant Goliath and later became a king. He is credited with writing Psalm 39 as well as many of the other psalms. David is the man the Lord told the prophet Samuel is "after his own heart" (1 Samuel 13:14). He was richly blessed in his life but was also a major screw-up at the same time. He spent a lot of time alone with God praying, singing, and worshiping. At points in his life, David recognized the blessings God provided. At other times, he went his own way, moved away from God, and inevitably suffered the consequences for his sin. Many of David's prayers are cries for help out of his sorrow, need for repentance, and desire for reconciliation with God. David gives us many examples of prayer and his desire for closeness and expression of thanks to God.

The Old Testament of the Bible contains many examples of prayer. During Jesus' life, the Scriptures were what we now call the Old Testament. What we call the New Testament was written after Jesus' ascension to heaven. It was these same Old Testament texts that Jesus studied as a youth. Jesus might have learned how to pray and of the importance of prayer from his scripture study. The same Scriptures that Jesus studied are available to us. Young Jesus could also have seen people pray at the temple during his visits there.

DID JESUS SEE HIS PARENTS PRAY?

As with any young person, parents have a major influence in life's direction. What role did Jesus' earthly parents have in his faith development?

Joseph was Jesus' earthly father. As with most fathers that are present in the lives of their children, Joseph would have been in a position to influence and teach Jesus.

Before Jesus was born, Joseph had a real dilemma. His bride-to-be, Mary, had become pregnant. Joseph knew it wasn't his child. Can you imagine the conversation that might have taken place between them? Nothing is recorded, but it might have gone like this.

Joseph: "Who's the father?"

Mary: "The Holy Spirit came over me and I became pregnant."

Joseph: "Really? I'm supposed to believe that?"

Mary: "Joseph, please! You must believe me!"

I could go on with that hypothetical dialogue but it wouldn't be pretty. Joseph probably felt as any man would when his fiancée seemingly betrayed him. He thought he'd do the noble thing and quietly break off the engagement so as to not disgrace her. Then as he slept, an angel appeared to him in a dream directing him to continue on with their wedding plans and confirmed Mary's story that this was a holy baby in her womb.

> *When Joseph woke up, he did as the angel of the Lord commanded and took Mary as his wife.* Matthew 1:24

The easy thing to do for Joseph would have been to continue with his plan. That's what I struggle with at times. It seems no matter what kind of direction or wise counsel I receive, I still struggle with submitting to it and taking the road less traveled, the hard road. Joseph took the hard road. It couldn't have been easy to agree to marry the pregnant, young woman. I wonder what his friends and family said to him about this.

Bottom line is that Joseph was faithful. He heard God's call and he answered. This is the kind of earthly father that raised Jesus from a baby to a man. Jesus had an earthy father that was faithful to his heavenly father and was courageous in answering his call.

How about Jesus' mother? What kind of earthly mother was she, and what might have Jesus learned and witnessed from his experience with her?

The gospel of Luke provides a great peek into Mary's spiritual life during her visit to her cousin Elizabeth. Both women were pregnant, Mary with Jesus and Elizabeth with John, who would become a messenger for Jesus, John the Baptist. Part of their conversation is recorded in Luke 1. Elizabeth greeted Mary upon arrival and was then filled with the Holy Spirit. This might have been when Elizabeth was given the revelation that Mary was carrying a special baby. She knew that Mary was "the mother of my Lord," (v. 43) and that Mary was blessed because of her faith. Mary's response gives us an idea of her faith.

Mary responded, "Oh, how my soul praises the Lord. How my spirit rejoices in God my Savior!" **Luke 1:46–47**

These verses are the beginning of Mary's song of praise found in Luke 1:46–55. What a beautiful expression by this young woman! Mary's song provides a look into her heart and shows the kind of young woman she was. We see her faith, her love for the Father, and her gratitude and her praise for him. This is the praise of a young woman, a teenager at the time, who was pregnant out of wedlock, without knowing any of the future for her or that of her son. She was simply faithful and grateful.

This is the heart of the mother of Jesus. This is the mother that raised him. The mother that cared for his needs, watched him grow, counseled him as a child, and followed him until his death on the cross and beyond. I wonder if Jesus prayed with his mother as a child. Scripture is silent on this. Seeing his mother's love for her Father in this passage, I wouldn't be surprised if she did.

HE PRAYED EARLY AND OFTEN

Jesus spent some of his prayer life in the presence of others.

> *"Pray like this: Our Father in heaven, may your name be kept holy. May your Kingdom come soon. May your will be done on earth, as it is in heaven. Give us today the food we need, and forgive us our sins, as we have forgiven those who sin against us. And don't let us yield to temptation, but rescue us from the evil one."* **Matthew 6:9–13**

Jesus prayed this prayer, the Lord's Prayer, during his time teaching his disciples. It seems he prayed aloud with them as a means of giving those listening a model for how to pray. It wasn't the only time Jesus prayed aloud with others, however it is the most widely known example. Here is another.

> *At that time Jesus prayed this prayer: "O Father, Lord of heaven and earth, thank you for hiding these things from those who think themselves wise and clever, and for revealing them to the childlike. Yes, Father, it pleased you to do it this way!"* **Matthew 11:25–26**

Jesus warned about praying aloud and with others in earshot.

> *"When you pray, don't be like the hypocrites who love to pray publicly on street corners and in the synagogues where everyone can see them. I tell you the truth, that is all the reward they will ever get."* **Matthew 6:5**

Is Jesus saying we shouldn't pray in public or with others? No. He's saying to not do so as the hypocrites do. Hypocrites only pretend to have the right beliefs but their behavior is not in alignment with those beliefs. He is saying we should pray with the right heart and out of sincerity. That's always how Jesus prayed.

Jesus also prayed alone.

> *After sending them home, he went up into the hills by himself to pray. Night fell while he was there alone.* Matthew 14:23

> *Before daybreak the next morning, Jesus got up and went out to an isolated place to pray.* Mark 1:35

Jesus spent long periods of time in solitude with his Father. There are several accounts of him rising before dawn to go off alone to pray. I wonder if while he was alone he prayed aloud. There is an account of Jesus praying in Luke 22. Jesus and the disciples had left the upper room where they had just finished what we know as the Last Supper. They headed to the Mount of Olives, which was a common place Jesus liked to pray. He walked away from the others about "a stone's throw," so maybe thirty yards or so, and knelt and prayed. What Jesus prayed is recorded.

> *"Father, if you are willing, please take this cup of suffering away from me. Yet I want your will to be done, not mine."* Luke 22:42

Since Jesus' prayer is recorded here, does it stand to reason that he might have been alone, away from the others, but prayed aloud? Perhaps.

YOUR WILL, NOT MINE

Here is another observation about the previous passage. Jesus asked his Father to take away the suffering that he knew was coming. He predicted his death on more than one occasion, and he seemed to know the time for this was drawing near. And then he expressed his desire to follow his Father's will and not his own. So is it that Jesus didn't get his way?

When I was fifteen years old, I had my driver's permit. My family would take regular trips back to the region my parents grew up, which was about a two and one-half-hour drive, much of it by freeway. We had a 1971 Ford Econoline van with no frills and no power steering. My dad let me drive home on one particular weekend with the family in the van. As we were going down the freeway, the van was veering back and forth, nearly violating the lane boundaries . . . not quite, but very close. I felt a stare coming from the passenger seat where my father was sitting. "What are you looking at?" he asked. "The road" I replied. "Where on the road?" he retorted. "Right in front of us!" I said. Then my dad gave me a lesson in not only driving, but one that I've worked to apply all my life. He explained that if I looked just barely over the hood, I would weave all over the road because my corrections would be too severe. But if I looked at the horizon, I would automatically make those small corrections necessary to keep me on track, without jolting too far to the left or right.

I tend to look just past the hood ornament in my life and not at the horizon. Then I overreact to what happens, and I try to jolt my life back into the center of the lane. God knows the big picture as his perspective is on eternity and not just what is happening in the moment. He knows the future. And he will make use of the challenges I have in the short term to develop me into the person he wants me to be for the future. His view is the long term. Actually, the longest term—forever.

Jesus was willing to look at the long term while praying in the garden. He knew God's perspective is perfect and that God knows what is best for him. So, after he asks for what he'd like to happen, he perfectly submitted to his Father's will: "Yet I want your will, not mine" (Luke 22:24).

DON'T GIVE UP, KEEP PRAYING!

Jesus taught us about the need for constant and persistent prayer.

He told a story of a widow who had been harmed. The judge dealing with the case was a bad guy, godless, and held contempt for everyone. The widow went to him over and over pleading her case. The judge ignored her at first, but finally relented and agreed to find justice for her.

> Then the Lord said, "Learn a lesson from this unjust judge. Even he rendered a just decision in the end. So don't you think God will surely give justice to his chosen people who cry out to him day and night? Will he keep putting them off?" Luke 18:6–7

The apostle Paul repeats this to the Thessalonians in his first letter to them.

> Always be joyful. Never stop praying. Be thankful in all circumstances, for this is God's will for you who belong to Christ Jesus. 1 Thessalonians 5:16–18

Jesus prayed often and persistently. He seemed to be in constant contact with the Father.

One of his beautiful prayers is in John 17. Jesus prayed to be glorified for the purpose of returning the glory back to the Father. He prayed for his disciples. Then, he offered this prayer for you and me.

> "I am praying not only for these disciples but also for all who will ever believe in me through their message." John 17:20

Wow . . . how does that make you feel? That Jesus prayed for you and me. He was concerned enough for us to bring his concerns to the Father on our behalf nearly two thousand years ago. That's mind-blowing for me!

So Jesus prayed. Did he need to? As one of the Godhead or Triune God (three in one) living as a man, would he have had a desire to communicate with the Father? Yes, he seemed to love to be in communication with God the Father.

Do you have someone you look forward to seeing again? When I travel away from home, I get excited to return when I know the trip is coming to an end. No matter how long the trip is, I seem to be able to sense the end coming. As I approach my street and make the turn toward my home, I get excited to see my family. I love to be home.

Jesus seemed to have this anticipation as well. He seemed enthusiastic to meet with the Father. He did this often and sometimes for long periods of time. We can learn much from Jesus prayer habits.

- Pray often and persistently.

- Pray sincerely, from the heart.

- Pray with others and alone.

- Be willing to pray aloud (even if you're alone).

- Pray for God's will.

- Lastly, pray in Jesus' name.

You can ask for anything in my name, and I will do it, so that the Son can bring glory to the Father. John 14:13

Thank you, Jesus that you gave us your life and these lessons in how to communicate with you. Amen.

STUDY QUESTIONS

1. What have you prayed for that you didn't get in the way you hoped? Are you yet able to see how God might have used this for your benefit (be honest, maybe not yet)?

2. Who has been a model for prayer in your life and what characteristics cause you to choose this person?

3. Think about your prayer "practice." What are your prayer habits (how, when, where)?

4. What are the characteristics of Jesus' prayer habits?

5. Which of Jesus' prayer habits come most natural to you? How about the ones you find most difficult?

CHAPTER ELEVEN

JESUS
FORGAVE

And Jesus replied, "I assure you, today you will be with me in paradise."
Luke 23:43

This chapter tackles a subject more difficult to define as a human characteristic than the previous ones. We certainly see forgiveness as the nature of God. Jesus both taught about forgiveness and acted out forgiveness during his earthly ministry. And forgiveness is also available to us in our humanity.

One of the first things learned in the journey to follow Jesus is that we are forgiven. It doesn't matter what we've done, to whom, how often, or how recent. When we turn our life and our will over to God with a sincere heart, he offers us the most gracious gift of unfathomable forgiveness. Awesome doesn't begin to describe how wonderful it is that God doesn't require restitution for each of the offenses we've committed. Can you imagine a penalty with varying weights depending on the gravity of the offense? Then we would have to serve our time based on what we've done. Sounds like our judicial system doesn't it?

WHAT? ME?

Think that wouldn't be a big deal? That you're a pretty good person? Consider that God knows every single thing you've done, thought, and considered. Every little white lie, stretch of the truth, and exaggeration you've offered to pump up yourself in the eyes of others. God knows every single time in your life that you've given a lusting glance at someone who's not your partner. And how about the times you've passed on stepping in to help someone in need when you're too busy to be inconvenienced? How about the time you walked out of the grocery store when you were given the wrong change? Then there's the angry glance at the driver trying to zipper into your lane in front of you. Seems like small stuff? I guess I didn't want to get too personal by bringing up any of what we seem to often think are the big screwups, but let's face it, we know what those were, don't we?

If you're like me, there wouldn't be enough time in my life to make up for all the things I've done wrong and pay restitution to those I've harmed in some way. And that doesn't even begin to address the unfortunate fact that even after beginning the journey to follow Jesus I continue to goof up and harm God and others. If God's ways were like that of our penal system, I'd be sunk. I'd keep losing ground every day with no possible way to make any headway.

Mercifully, God knows this and allows us to hit the reset button on our lives. We can have decades of living our lives on our terms, come to him humbly, ask forgiveness, and we're washed as clean as snow. And we're afforded the opportunity to do this again and again for the remainder of our lives so long as our hearts are genuine. That's God's way.

> *"Though your sins are like scarlet, I will make them as white as snow. Though they are red like crimson, I will make them as white as wool."* Isaiah 1:18b

BY THE BOOK

The definition of the word *forgive* from Merriam-Webster is "to stop feeling anger" or "to stop blaming" someone who has done something wrong.[1] An alternative definition from Wikipedia reads "the intentional and voluntary process by which a victim undergoes a change in feelings and attitude regarding an offense, lets go of negative emotions such as vengefulness, with an increased ability to wish the offender well."[2] So by these definitions, God stops feeling anger or blaming us for things by which we have victimized him. I guess I've never thought of God as being a victim before. I'm having a hard time embracing this, but I can see that he has been harmed by our sin.

> *The Lord observed the extent of human wickedness on the earth, and he saw that everything they thought or imagined was consistently and totally evil. So the Lord was sorry he had ever made them and put them on the earth. It broke his heart. And the Lord said, "I will wipe this human race I have created from the face of the earth. Yes, and I will destroy every living thing—all the people, the large animals, the small animals that scurry along the ground, and even the birds of the sky. I am sorry I ever made them."* **Genesis 6:5–8**

Right from the beginning of recorded human history, God was sorry that he created us because our response to him was disobedience. God is our creator and the giver of all good things, yet we continue to choose to do things our own way. We ignore God's instruction and distance ourselves from him.

LESSONS ON FORGIVENESS

In the gospel of Matthew within the story of the Sermon on the Mount, Jesus provided direction on how to deal with someone who is angry with you.

> *"So if you are presenting a sacrifice at the altar in the Temple and you suddenly remember that someone has something against you,*

leave your sacrifice there at the altar. Go and be reconciled to that
person. Then come and offer your sacrifice to God." Matthew 5:23-24

Jesus seemed to be placing a priority on forgiveness before the sacrifice to God that Jews so faithfully made. I wonder how radical an idea
this must have been, to make things right with another person before
going to the temple. But this seems to be God's instruction as Jesus
directed us to do this.

Continuing with the Sermon on the Mount, Jesus offered his instruction on how to handle matters when *you* are the one being offended.
The previous lesson dealt with when we're the cause, but in this case,
here's what he said on how to handle things when we've been harmed.

"If you forgive those who sin against you, your heavenly Father
will forgive you. But if you refuse to forgive others, your Father
will not forgive your sins." Matthew 6:14-15

Tough teaching by Jesus. The Father asks of us only to do what he does
for us. Our offenses to God are deep and numerous. Yet God is willing
to forgive again and again. God is merciful. He requires the same of
us. We may find this difficult at times, but it is the right response to
our faith. When we've felt forgiveness, especially the absolute kind
offered by God, we are apt to forgive as well.

On one occasion Peter approached Jesus and asked him how often
should he forgive someone. Have you ever thought that? You've been
wronged over and over and over by someone. At some point, aren't we
just allowed to remain angry with them and not let it go?

Then Peter came to him and asked, "Lord, how often should I for-
give someone who sins against me? Seven times?" "No, not seven
times," Jesus replied, "but seventy times seven!" Matthew 18:21-22

Jesus then followed this with an illustration of a servant who owed a
huge amount of money to the king and was unable to pay. The king

showed mercy on him and let him off the hook. The servant's response? When a fellow servant couldn't pay his debt back to the forgiven servant, he had him arrested until the debt could be paid. When the king found out, he then did the same to the servant to whom he had originally provided relief. Jesus said this will happen to us if we don't forgive.

Jesus likely didn't mean to offer forgiveness specifically 490 times (70 times 7 if you didn't catch that). We are to forgive as we've been forgiven. Do you think God has forgiven you more than 490 times? How about a lot more? So, what should be our response to acknowledging God's forgiveness of us?

Back to the Sermon on the Mount. Is there a reward for forgiving another? God tells us that he will bless us when we show mercy to others. God's mercy is most valuable as it provides us a sense of peace and community with him as we begin to feel it and believe it is available to us.

> *"God blesses those who are merciful, for they will be shown mercy."*
> Matthew 5:7

HEALING, LOVE, AND FORGIVENESS

Several encounters Jesus had with others during his three-year recorded ministry involve physical healing as well as critical conversations with people about their lives and struggles. One encounter involved a paralyzed man who was desperate to see Jesus. He had four buddies who lowered him through an opening in the roof, as the dwelling in which Jesus stood was too crowded for them to get close.

> *Seeing their faith, Jesus said to the paralyzed man, "My child, your sins are forgiven."* Mark 2:5

The first order of business was forgiveness. Jesus also healed the man's paralysis, but only after this man had been set free from his past mistakes.

In another series of events, Jesus was offered a meal at one of the Pharisee's homes. This man would have been a religious leader and possibly set on maintaining the status quo, meaning not giving consideration to Jesus, his teaching, and claims about himself. I imagine the scene as a roomy area where people were coming and going—servants and the like—not like a modern dinner party we'd have in our private home today. Jesus showed up, was greeted by the host, chitchatted with the other guests, and joined the group to enjoy the dinner. Then an immoral woman entered the room. She knelt before Jesus, started crying, then poured perfume on his feet, and wiped his feet with her hair. The washing of feet before a meal was common hygiene, but having a prostitute do it for you was likely not cool.

The Pharisees thought Jesus was unaware of her profession and, if he did know, he should not allow her to touch him, at least not if the claims about him were true. Jesus gave them a lesson on the gravity of sin when he compared the Pharisee's response to Jesus to how the woman poured out herself over him. She knew her sins, and she knew she was forgiven. The weight of forgiven sins was counterbalanced by love of the forgiver.

> "I tell you, her sins—and they are many—have been forgiven, so she has shown me much love. But a person who is forgiven little shows only little love." Luke 7:47

Her response wasn't significant because her sin was so much greater than that of the Pharisee. Her response was significant because she understood and felt the great forgiveness of God as the great forgiver.

MODEL FOR PRAYER AND COMMUNION

Jesus gave a lesson to the disciples on prayer. Common practice for the time would be to pray loud and proud, do it in public so that everyone could see that the person was praying. I guess one was supposed to get credit for that somehow. Jesus urged that when we pray to do it between God and ourselves. It is a private conversation requiring candor and honesty, not boasting and bragging.

The Lord's Prayer was given directly by Jesus to those early disciples. He left us with this as a template to follow for the things we ought to cover with God in our communication with him. Interestingly, in this short little prayer, Jesus covers forgiveness. So few topics are dealt with in this brief prayer, yet Jesus decided that among all that could be prayed for and about, forgiveness was one.

> *"And forgive us our sins, as we have forgiven those who sin against us."* **Matthew 6:12**

Later, at what we now call the Last Supper, Jesus officiated at the first communion among his closest disciples. He gave us the symbolism of his body and the bread as well as his blood and the wine. The forgiveness theme is central to communion. Jesus foreshadowed his execution that was necessary for our forgiveness and salvation.

> *For this is my blood, which confirms the covenant between God and his people. It is poured out as a sacrifice to forgive the sins of many."* **Matthew 26:28**

HUMAN FORGIVENESS

At the beginning of this chapter, I acknowledged that studying the topic of forgiveness as it relates to the humanity of Jesus is a complicated subject, perhaps more so than the other human characteristics that Jesus exhibited. Most of the other characteristics don't necessarily seem to be so God-like as forgiveness. To forgive, you must first be harmed. We've harmed God, as mentioned earlier, so God is in the position to forgive us. God is in the place where he is the only one that can forgive us. After all, the harm we've caused was to him. But does he have the propensity to forgive us? Does God have the inclination or motivation to do this? Yes, God does, because he loves us and forgives us with no strings attached when asked sincerely.

As for Jesus, how and when was he harmed in his manhood so that his forgiveness would flow from his humanity?

Consider the mind-blowing forgiveness offered by Jesus on the cross. We mostly know the scene—Jesus taken into custody, abandoned by his friends and followers, beaten by his captors, imprisoned, whipped, humiliated, and then led out to carry his own cross to his execution. As he hung on the cross, exasperated as his lungs were collapsing under the weight of his own hanging torso, he found a way to say aloud so those in attendance could hear that he forgave his executioners.

Jesus said, "Father, forgive them, for they don't know what they are doing." Luke 23:34

I can think of nothing that compares to this scene. Jesus, while in physical pain from the inhumane beatings and torture, then displayed his gracious forgiveness, freely given to those not requesting it. This hardly seems possible to me that one could forgive those oppressing and murdering him right during the time of the act itself. This example of forgiveness surpasses all that I think is possible, except that it really did happen. Can you imagine doing that? Truthfully I can't imagine doing this myself. I know with God's strength, anything is possible. I would certainly need to rely on his strength and ability to forgive, as I don't have this capacity on my own.

OTHER WORLDLY FORGIVENESS

On October 2, 2006, a lone gunman entered a one-room Amish schoolhouse in a small Pennsylvania town, murdering many of the pupils and critically injuring others before turning the gun on himself. When interviewed, the parents of the slain children offered words of forgiveness and comfort for the perpetrator's widow and her three children. Forgiveness became the big story, reaching all the major news outlets. Following their own kids' burials, the victims' parents made up half the seventy-five attendees at the murderer's own funeral.

If that wasn't enough, the Amish families set up a fund to support the shooter's family.[3]

Amazing grace, how sweet the sound. I love it when in the face of tragedy we have the opportunity to peer into someone's life who is living in God's inconceivable mercy and grace. The reason this behavior makes the news is because it doesn't make sense. If you're operating in the paradigm of this world, a response like this isn't logical. Actually it's not a logic response; it's a Jesus-like response. Most of the world doesn't understand that. Jesus didn't follow the logic of the world.

Jesus forgave. He forgave others' sins when he healed them. He taught on the importance of forgiveness and the results for us when we forgive others. He showed us the greatest example of forgiveness from the cross. We've seen examples of extraordinary forgiveness in more recent times. How about you? Are you hanging onto a grudge right now? Is it time to let it go and consider the forgiveness that God has offered you? Can you still really hold onto your resentment after you come to the realization that God's done immeasurably more for you than he's asking from you?

STUDY QUESTIONS

1. Do you have someone in your life whom you have had a difficult time forgiving? Think carefully and put his or her initials here.

2. How was it possible for the Amish community to forgive their children's murderer?

3. Make a brief list of blessings God has provided for you—that you know you didn't earn and don't necessarily deserve.

4. Have you ever stolen, lied, cheated, been selfish, or experienced unrighteous anger? Just a simply "yes" or "no" will do.

5. Are you forgiven? Have you been blessed in your life? Can you now pray for God to help you forgive the person in question number one above?

amazed

JESUS
CARRIED HIS CROSS

Carrying the cross by himself, he went to the place called Place of the Skull (in Hebrew, Golgotha). John 19:17

In Jesus' case, the saying "carried his cross" has both a metaphorical meaning as well as being something he physically did. I'd like to suggest another way to view this saying. First let's examine the physical act.

Jesus was betrayed by Judas in the Garden of Gethsemane and turned over to the Roman and temple guard through the identifying kiss Judas placed on Jesus' cheek. A "contingent of Roman soldiers" (John 18:3) or a detachment of about six hundred men was sent to collect Jesus. I know Jesus had his own posse, but this seems like a major overreaction to me. I guess they weren't taking any chances.

Once Jesus was restrained, he was taken in for questioning by several people. He was led to Annas (high priest Caiaphas's father-in-law),

Caiaphas and other leading priests, the entire high council or Sanhedrin, and finally to Pontius Pilate, along with a brief interrogation by Herod Antipas, the ruler from Galilee who happened to be visiting the region at the time.

Pilate, having the lead political role in the trial of Jesus, seemed to want nothing to do with the situation. It appeared he saw this as a problem for the Jews, as the offense by Jesus seemed to be more of a religious problem than a political one. Pilate was all about politics, self-promotion, and self-preservation as well as keeping the peace. Keeping the peace *was* his main means of self-preservation.

In order to appease the crowd, Pilate had Jesus flogged with a lead-tipped whip. The soldiers then wedged a thorny crown upon Jesus' head as a way of mocking his claim to be a king. He was punched, spit upon, and ridiculed by his captors. After the beating of thirty-nine lashes with the whip, Jesus likely had pieces of flesh hanging from his back and would have been bleeding badly. Blood and sweat caused from the crown of thorns might have run into his eyes causing difficulty seeing and creating a painful sting. When the robe placed on him by the guards was removed so that his clothes could be placed back on him again, it might have felt like tearing off a bandage that had dried into a blood-crusted wound, initiating the cycle of pain all over again.

Pilate made the fateful decision to have Jesus executed by crucifixion and turned him over to the guards. Jesus was then led to Golgotha, or Skull Hill, to be put to death. He would have been sleep deprived, bloody, bruised, and in constant physical pain. The loss of blood from the earlier beating might also have weakened him. Then the heavy wooden crossbeam that would complete the cross when joined to the upright post was placed on his shoulders. The crosspiece, or *patibulum*, probably weighed between thirty and forty pounds. It's not known how far the trek was to Skull Hill but estimates range from .2 to .33 miles.[1] A quarter mile would be a reasonable average of these estimates—meaning the distance would have been a little more than the length of four football fields. Imagine being tired and not feeling well (to say the least), and it's hot and dusty with the sun beating down.

Now consider placing a bag of water softener salt on your shoulders and walk up and down a football field its full length several times. This is not really a fair comparison of the difficult journey Jesus faced, but considering this illustration gives a little context for his experience.

Yet it was our weaknesses he carried; it was our sorrows that weighed him down. And we thought his troubles were a punishment from God, a punishment for his own sins! But he was pierced for our rebellion, crushed for our sins. He was beaten so we could be whole. He was whipped so we could be healed. Isaiah 53:4–5

CULTURAL ICON

The symbol of the cross is extraordinarily simple to create. Draw a vertical line. Now draw a second line intersecting the first at a right angle (or perpendicular to the first line) with the bisecting point occurring about a third of the way down from the top of the first or vertical line. There, you've now drawn a cross. See, simple.

Variations of the cross have been used for a variety of means and by different organizations over the years. Military groups have used a version of the cross in their symbolism. The Nazi party, when formed in early twentieth century, adopted its version of a cross with the swastika.[2] Motorcycle and inner city gangs have adopted the cross as part of their emblems. Check out Celtic icons to see how an entire culture has taken on the cross to represent its heritage. The cross has become pervasive in our world. Look at jewelry and tattoos to see what symbols are in vogue now. All of these groups are not necessarily following Jesus' lead on what the cross means, although some may. Don't judge the tattooed biker too quickly.

A NEW KING FOR THE KNOWN WORLD

During Jesus' time living as a man on earth, the disciples seemed not to understand the context for the kingdom Jesus came to set up. Jesus talked often about his kingdom, and even late in his three-year earthly ministry, he became very pointed and almost obvious about his plan and intentions. We do have to cut the disciples some slack. The Jews, including Jesus' disciples, had read in scripture and been taught that the Messiah would be coming. The event was often predicted in the Old Testament, which would have been their key reference material. Each of the previous historical kings set up shop on earth. And with the continued, escalating Roman rule oppressing the occupants of Jerusalem each day, the time seemed ripe for another king—the king who had been foretold, who would bring peace and save the Jews from oppression. They were ready for a new world order.

The crowd was listening to everything Jesus said. And because he was nearing Jerusalem, he told them a story to correct the impression that the Kingdom of God would begin right away. Luke 19:11

Following the above passage, Jesus told a parable about ten servants. The king gave each servant the same amount of money. The first couple of servants reporting back have recorded good gains from the investments they had made, while the next servant hid the money given to him so it wouldn't be lost. A key learning is that we are to make good use of the gifts, talents, and resources God gives us. And the big message is about the judgment of the king. Here, Jesus foreshadows the future for his listening audience.

There is no record of any reaction his followers might have had to Jesus' message about the servants. Maybe they still didn't get it.

Jesus came to set up a new order for the world. Or perhaps to move us toward the way in which the world was originally designed by the Father. He didn't intend to set up his kingdom in the conventional manner. It would be a new world order with Jesus making all the rules.

FURTHER FORESHADOWING

Jesus didn't come to win a popularity contest. He came to save us from sin and eternal separation from God. Several recorded things that were said by Jesus seemed to actually cause him to lose followers when he spoke to them.

> *"The Son of Man must suffer many terrible things," he said. "He will be rejected by the elders, the leading priests, and the teachers of religious law. He will be killed, but on the third day he will be raised from the dead."* Luke 9:22

This was spoken in such plain language it is hard to believe Jesus was not understood. Yet time and time again, his followers questioned him; their actions seemed to indicate they didn't grasp the mission. They continued to hope for the earthly ruler who would unseat the Roman government. Punctuating the confusion is the parallel account in Matthew 16:22 that has Peter declaring, "Heaven forbid, Lord . . . this will never happen to you!" Peter didn't get it. Not yet, anyway. As with the other disciples, he would later.

With the benefit of hindsight, we understand the following in the context of knowing how Jesus' earthly mission played out.

> *Then he said to the crowd, "If any of you wants to be my follower, you must turn from your selfish ways, take up your cross daily, and follow me."* Luke 9:23

I have often wondered when Jesus talked about shouldering one's cross if that meant anything to his followers. They were certainly aware of the crucifixion method used by the Romans, but did they have any idea how to apply what Jesus said? Funny, even though we seem to be able to put this into context today, we find the message of carrying our cross one that is difficult to grasp and even harder to do.

Jesus physical body was put to death on the cross. This is not only a documented historical fact but is also the climactic metaphor for Jesus' teachings. Cross = Death. That's the lesson. Whenever Jesus mentions the cross he's referring to death.

DENIAL OF SELF

Left to our own devices and ambitions, many of us would make most of our decisions in our own favor and perhaps at times at the expense of others.

Have you ever cut into a "zipper" lane on the freeway ahead of a driver that seemed to be attempting to pinch you out? Small thing, but what is it about driving that seems to bring out the worst in us? We want what we want when we want it.

Jesus' call for "death" is to deny our own desires and place his desires first. Oftentimes the way we live this out is by putting other people first. How about letting the next driver zippering in next to you go ahead of you? Jesus demonstrated the denial of self in his prayer just prior to his arrest in the garden. I know it's a small thing, but isn't this an example of denying our own desires and placing another's ahead of our own? Selflessness?

> *He went on a little farther and bowed with his face to the ground, praying, "My Father! If it is possible, let this cup of suffering be taken away from me. Yet I want your will to be done, not mine."*
> Matthew 26:39

We have so much to learn from this short prayer. It seems Jesus was humble and in anguish over the thought of the forthcoming events. He stated his desire—let this cup of suffering be taken away from me. Then he affirmed that his Father's will was what mattered. God the Father's will was the priority. And ultimately, Jesus submitted and followed. I seem too often to take the easier, softer way. Jesus took the hard road because he knew it was the Father's will.

Think of the title to an automobile. It's a piece of paper that looks very official. It contains the specifics of the make, model, and mileage at time of transfer as well as if there are any loans on the car and, most importantly, who owns the car. In most cases, when the title is signed, the document becomes a live document, meaning whoever possesses the title actually owns the car. The holder of the signed title can take possession of the car, resell the car, drive the car, scrap the car, or do anything else he or she wants. Until the title is signed, the car is still owned by the person named on the title. Once signed, the title may then be turned over to a new owner.

We all have the title to our lives. We own our lives, or at least we mostly act as though we do. We make decisions every day that reflect our ownership—eat what we decide to eat, go where we decide to go, and do what we decide to do. By agreeing to deny ourselves, Jesus is urging us to sign the title of our lives and hand it over to him. He'll decide what he'll have us do, and we'll follow because we no longer have ownership of our lives.

My friend Dave has lived this out for several years. Jesus gave him a heart of compassion for the homeless in our community. Dave was inspired to begin serving a simple breakfast outside of a homeless shelter in Minneapolis. Each day, every day, he began with preparations starting around 4:30 a.m. with clean up ending at 7:00 a.m. He felt compassion for others and was moved to serve. After beginning this ministry, several others have been inspired and have joined the effort. I think Jesus holds the signed title of Dave's life.

COMPLETE SUBMISSION

One definition for submission is "the action or fact of accepting or yielding to a superior force or to the will or authority of another person."[3] Jesus submitted to the Father in his prayer at the Garden of Gethsemane. He acknowledged that he wanted to do God's will and not his own. Jesus yielded to the Father's plan.

Why would we submit to anyone?

I guided a canoe trip in the Boundary Waters Canoe Area Wilderness in northern Minnesota many years ago. It was my first time as the lead guide on a trip, although I had been on trips several times before. We put in off the Echo Trail onto the Little Indian Sioux River and paddled south for about half a day. The problem was that we should have traveled north on the river. When I peeked at the map as we were putting our gear in the canoes, I interpreted the map backwards and led us in exactly the opposite direction we were supposed to travel. It took several hours for me to come to grips with the idea that we might be lost. Fortunately, we encountered a couple of other travelers, and when I asked them to show me where we were on the map, my error was uncovered. Rather than continue to follow my own way, I trusted their direction; we turned around and paddled back toward where we came from, which was the right direction.

We tend to submit to someone else when we're in trouble, lost, or sense that we need help. That may be why so many testimonies of Jesus' followers have a climactic moment where life really goes sideways and the willingness to reach out for help and submit to God becomes the solution.

> *And I know that nothing good lives in me, that is, in my sinful nature. I want to do what is right, but I can't. I want to do what is good, but I don't. I don't want to do what is wrong, but I do it anyway. But if I do what I don't want to do, I am not really the one doing wrong; it is sin living in me that does it.* Romans 7:18–20

The author here is the apostle Paul, one of the notable spiritual giants of scripture. It sounds like he's giving himself a pretty good beating when it comes to trusting himself, his own desires, and his ability to get things right on his own. Paul points to the one solution for his, and our, condition—submission to Jesus.

DEATH

Death is the ultimate sacrifice. Jesus experienced death in his physical body for us as the penalty for sin. There was no escaping it, and Jesus knew it. Either we pay or he does. He lived the perfect, sin-free life. This qualified him to pay the price for us—and he did.

Who among us would not have taken ourselves down from that cross or stopped the beatings, ridiculing, punching, and being spat upon if we knew we had the power to do it? I squirm and whine in the dentist's chair when I feel the slightest bit of pain. If I knew of another way to get my dental work done without the possibility of experiencing any pain, I'd do it in a heartbeat. And yet Jesus willingly submitted to the pain, and even though he knew he had the power to stop the proceedings at any moment, he chose not to. That was the Father's will and he knew it. Jesus understood his purpose and mission, and even through the debilitating torture he looked neither left nor right but rather looked straight into the eyes of the Father, and said, "It is finished!" (John 19:30).

> *"I tell you the truth, unless a kernel of wheat is planted in the soil and dies, it remains alone. But its death will produce many new kernels—a plentiful harvest of new lives. Those who love their life in this world will lose it. Those who care nothing for their life in this world will keep it for eternity."* John 12:24–25

There are many paradoxes in life. Isn't it curious that in the design of plant life, some of the seeds that have the ability to be converted into nourishing food for us must be set aside and allowed to die? Then, at some later time, these same seeds are planted again, spring into life as plants, and the seeds are multiplied in abundance. The dead seed brings new life. As we die to self, submit to the will of the Father, and follow his agenda rather than our own, God will use us to create a plentiful harvest. So, dying is not so bad after all!

LIVING IN ME

The apostle Paul sums up the death discussion in this chapter better than I ever could.

> *My old self has been crucified with Christ. It is no longer I who live, but Christ lives in me. So I live in this earthly body by trusting in the Son of God, who loved me and gave himself for me.*
> Galatians 2:20

Paul didn't consider himself alive any longer except that he lived through Jesus who lived in him. That's a promise. Jesus will come to us in our death. When we decide to submit our lives to him, give up our agenda and follow him, Jesus is the death to our previous lives. Only then can we be reborn into a new life, one in which Jesus becomes the center.

Jesus carried his cross and we can too. This doesn't mean we have a burden in our life that we have to endure. Sure, life can be tough, but I'm not sure that's what he meant. Rather, I think he meant the carrying of our cross is our willingness to do what Jesus did. Jesus denied himself and followed the Father's plan, he submitted his will to the Father's, and he died the death we deserve.

Can you follow God's will, submit to his plan, and "die" to this life for the life he has planned for you? Following Jesus is a real adventure. Believe me, he's got a wild plan in store just for you.

STUDY QUESTIONS

1. What symbols of the cross do you have in your home, office, car, or on your person?

2. Describe the most physically challenging task you've ever done.

3. Tell of a time when you experienced your most physical pain or trauma. Would you have avoided it if you possibly could?

4. Talk about a situation when you really needed help from someone else.

5. In the case of question number four, what was it that caused you to ask for help from this particular person or organization? Did they have knowledge, experience, or resources that gave you confidence that they would be able to help you?

amazed

CONCLUSION

think the joke is on me. As a matter of fact, I'm pretty sure it is. As I've gone through the process of writing this book, it's taken me a year. I realize it isn't a very long book, but I'm a busy guy. And I'm not a professional writer—if that wasn't obvious already.

In the two years leading up to this project, I was inspired to read the gospels, the first four books in the New Testament in the Bible: Matthew, Mark, Luke, and John. I was beginning a journey in my life in which I wanted to know Jesus better. In the gospels, Jesus is alive as a man, he's quoted literally, and I could follow his life here on earth—at least the parts that are written down. I love Jesus, and like anyone I love, I want to spend more time with that person. Think about the early stages of a boyfriend/girlfriend relationship. Don't you just want to spend all your time with him or her?

The best way I could find to spend time with Jesus was to read the gospels. I don't know how many times I read them through, but when I'd get to the end of John, I'd start over again with Matthew. And so on. During my reading I noticed some of the actions, feelings, and experiences Jesus had that seemed human and not so God-like. It was a curious observation, and I'm not the first one to notice this.

To expand my knowledge about scripture, I would often look to other sources. I tried to research the author or compiler so I could trust that the source was reliable. Anything that seemed quirky to me, I tried to dig deeper into scripture to confirm, or I took my question to one of my pastors. I looked for material I could read on Jesus living out his humanity. I did find a couple of other books but wasn't satisfied with my search results.

Then it hit me while I was mowing my lawn—I can literally point out the spot in my yard where it happened—I've got to write this book.

So the joke is that when I tell people that I'm writing a book, they seem a little surprised, especially those who know me well. The line goes like this, "I didn't want to write a book, I just wanted to read a book, but it hasn't been written yet." That's the joke. But God gets the last laugh.

The process of writing this book has helped me in getting to know Jesus better. I've held countless conversations on the topic of Jesus' humanity with friends, acquaintances, pastors, and anyone else that I can coax into a conversation on the topic. Although I don't give specific credit to any one individual for their specific idea in the book, believe me when I say that some of what is written has been shaped and influenced by others who have great observations and intriguing questions about Jesus and his time living as one of us.

On the topic of credibility, I considered the source of any material I read before adopting the ideas. I am not a pastor and have no formal theological training. As I said, I also don't consider myself a professional author. So if you consider the source and had read this section of the book first, you might have stopped and read no further. That's why I put this at the end of the book.

Stylistically, I aimed to wonder aloud and ask more questions than I give answers. I'm not the most qualified to answer those questions anyway. But I do wonder about things, and I do like to ask questions. I have tried to suggest things and urge readers to consider things. And I do suggest a conclusion from time to time; however, I have attempted to restrain myself from stating too many closed-ended conclusions whenever I lack the specific knowledge to do so.

In the event you find something that you are clear on that I've stated is untrue, incorrect, or doesn't follow your understanding of theology, please reach out to me and point out your finding. You can reach me through my blog at www.richardbahr.com.

Above all, I want you to know Jesus. This book is not aimed at someone who has no belief in Jesus, although I don't rule that out completely. Additionally I did not write this in such a heady fashion that real theologians or academics would likely find interesting. If you are one of them, I suggest you skim this book then give it to someone that you think would find it helpful.

To know Jesus. That's the goal. To know him as our friend, our Lord, our Savior, our counselor, our guide, our inspiration, our strength, the giver of all good gifts, and as our redeemer. That's my hope. My hope is that this book may play some small part in helping you get to know the Jesus that I'm beginning to know.

Jesus is your friend. He can relate to you. You can relate to him. He understands. He lived just as you do. Why not trust him now? You have everything to gain.

Acknowledgments

I did a terrible job keeping track of all of the people who influenced and stimulated me in my thinking while I was developing this book. The truth is, I enjoyed the conversations so much it didn't occur to me to keep track. So those of you that know me and were drawn into a conversation about Jesus' humanity during the development of this book, you know who you are. And thank you.

Both Nathan Kemper and Tim Magnuson reviewed my manuscript during its development. Nate read early versions of the first three chapters as well as provided an endorsement for this book. And Tim did a most through job of not only editing punctuation but helping in several other elements including explaining the difference in the use of the term "apostle" versus "disciple." I enjoyed our review of this work and thank both men for the time they generously provided.

Jennifer Leonardson has helped support my core business's marketing effort through her business Oxyjen Design (www.oxyjendesign.com) for many years. I really like her work. I can toss out an idea and she can bring it to life. Jen was willing to work with us on this project to come up with the cover design for the book. Thanks.

Jessica Ess led the way for the interior design of the book and typesetting. This was an important final touch that really helps to bring the book to life. Thank you.

Susan Niemi, working through Huff Publishing, really made this book better. She's a stickler on the use of tense but most importantly helped me state my points in ways that would be inclusive and not leave anyone out. I would never want someone to feel left out because of my writing when God may have a message for someone in this work. Thanks, Susan, for being willing to work with a rookie.

My wife, Carla, supported my time spent on this work. I spent many hours typing and researching rather than engaged with her on things she would most certainly enjoy more than listening to my keyboard. Then, when the rough manuscript was completed she encouraged me to see the publishing through rather than post it as an e-book on line for free, which was my idea. You're the best.

Finally, I pitched this concept to Bill Huff over a year before having a manuscript ready for submission. Bill read my first three chapters and encouraged me to continue. He told me he didn't know of anything quite like this and urged me to pursue it. At least that's what I heard. However he really said it, it worked to inspire me to see it through. Thank you.

NOTES

CHAPTER 2: JESUS HONORED HIS MOTHER

1. Charles Spurgeon's quote from "Got Questions" website at http://www.gotquestions.org/age-of-accountability.html. This same quote was on several websites, all attributed to Spurgeon.

2. David H. Stern. *Jewish New Testament Commentary*. Jewish New Testament Publications, Inc., 1992. Kindle edition, location 1457.

3. *A Complete Bible Reference Study Library* (4 in 1): KJV Bible with Strong's markup, Strong's Concordance & Dictionaries, Lexicon Definitions, and Bible word index. Bestbooks, 2015. Kindle edition, location 257521.

CHAPTER 3: JESUS WAS TEMPTED

1. Bruce A. Ware. *The Man Christ Jesus: Theological Reflections on the Humanity of Christ*. Wheaton, IL: Crossway, 2013. Kindle edition, location 1106.

2. Ray Stedman's website at http://www.raystedman.org/thematic-studies/the-life-of-christ/the-temptation-of-christ.

CHAPTER 6: JESUS WAS AMAZED

1. Encyclopedia Britannica website, http://www.britannica.com/topic/centurion-Roman-military-officer.

CHAPTER 7: JESUS WEPT

1. Although there were about 600,000 residents at the time of the city's destruction, since this tragic event occurred during the Passover celebration at which many Jews made their pilgrimage to the temple, it is thought there might have been about 1,000,000 victims during the fall of Jerusalem. More information can be found in several places. A summary of the history of the population of Jerusalem can be found at the Wikipedia website at https://en.wikipedia.org/wiki/Historical_Jewish_population_comparisons.

2. Pastor Greg Laurie's blog on his website Jesus.org at http://www.jesus.org/death-and-resurrection/holy-week-and-passion/why-did-jesus-weep-during-the-triumphal-entry.html.

CHAPTER 8: JESUS WAS ANGRY

1. Merriam-Webster's online dictionary at http://www.merriam-webster.com/dictionary/.

2. Ibid.

CHAPTER 9: JESUS SERVED

1. Albert Nolan. *Jesus before Christianity.* Orbis Books, 1976, 1992, 2001. Kindle edition, p. 4e.

2. Philip Yancey. *The Jesus I Never Knew.* Zondervan, 2008. Kindle Edition, p. 191.

3. Ibid, 232.

CHAPTER 11: JESUS FORGAVE

1. Merriam-Webster's online dictionary at http://www.merriam-webster.com/dictionary/forgive.

2. Wikipedia, at https://en.wikipedia.org/wiki/Forgiveness.

3. This tragic event was covered by worldwide media outlets. Summary from Wikipedia at https://en.wikipedia.org/wiki/West_Nickel_Mines_School_shooting.

CHAPTER 12: JESUS CARRIED HIS CROSS

1. The exact route Jesus traveled to Golgotha or Skull Hill is not known. I did an Internet search and compared the distances listed on several sites to determine the estimated range. The precise distance is not the significant issue; it's about Jesus' journey to the execution place taken after the beatings he received as well as the size and weight of the cross he carried. Any distance traveled under these conditions would have been excruciating.

2. The swastika has a long history going back thousands of years. The Nazi party took this on as their own symbol during the rise in power of Adolf Hitler. More on its history can be found at the United States Holocaust Memorial Museum's website at http://www.ushmm.org/wlc/en/article.php?ModuleId=10007453.

3. Oxford Dictionary at http://www.oxforddictionaries.com/us/definition/american_english/submission.

The beginning of Threshold to New Life

Have you experienced a defining moment in your life? One during which you knew that's what it might actually be? Most of us with any time on this earth have sensed this. Some of these are traumatic circumstances. An event happens after which you know life will never be the same. Loss of a loved one may cause this feeling . . . or an uplifting event such as a wedding or birth of a child, especially the first child.

My wife, Carla, and I had such an experience together. We didn't mean to. It wasn't bad either. It just happened.

The small group we were leading finished reading the book *Radical* by David Platt, and we felt really challenged by what Platt describes as a radical faith in Jesus. As Carla and I discussed the book ahead of one of our last small group meetings, she said to me something like, "We need to do something." I asked, "Like what?" She replied, "I don't know for sure. But the work you're doing with the homeless now, we should get that organized." Organized? I'm still not sure that I connected with that term at the time, but I have learned since what "organized" can mean.

I had been serving in a breakfast ministry at a local homeless shelter for the previous five years. I would go one or two mornings per week, help with food prep, serve the breakfast, and as time permitted, visit with the clients. Because I was regular, I got to know many of the folks we served. Soon I earned the privilege of hearing about their struggles, fears, and frustrations. Along with this I listened to their hopes and aspirations. I really felt like these folks were becoming my friends.

When I was out of town and unable to attend, I actually would miss getting up at 4:00 a.m. to go serve. I missed the interaction and connection with the people I was learning to care about.

I learned about some of the gaps in my new friends' lives—things such as a needed article of clothing, a bus fare, a ride to a doctor appointment, or an application fee for housing. These seemed like small things to me but made a great deal of difference to my friends. That's when the stakes started to go up.

We got involved in a few housing cases, helping to secure housing and funding part of the deposit or first month's rent. We learned quickly that the people who do this all the time are well connected and know how to find places efficiently. We didn't, but still wanted to help.

That's where getting "organized" came in.

Carla had a vision for how we might not only give from what God has blessed us with, but also serve right alongside, stepping into the gaps in people's lives. So we sat down that weekend, drafted a mission and vision, picked an anchoring Bible verse, and discussed who might want to be involved. Importantly we prayed. We needed God's leading in this, otherwise there's really no reason to do it.

So we launched Threshold to New Life in the spring of 2013. We asked a few people to join us; we set up a website and got an email address, phone number, and some business cards. We were in business.

The temporal needs that I run into at the shelters I frequent continue. I buy lots of socks as well as winter items—jackets, gloves, and hats—and take special orders for shoes and whatever else is needed. We did get involved in a few more housing cases and helped as best we knew how.

Somehow, none of us seem to remember, we got connected to one of the housing programs that is affiliated with a homeless shelter—many shelters are affiliated housing programs. The idea is to move people through the shelters and into permanent housing. At least that's the idea. My experience is different. There are many people I personally watched live in shelters for years at a time, often times having "permanent" housing in their recent past. The reasons these individuals are in shelters are numerous. Some are in part brought on by the people themselves, and many are not. It's complicated. Let's just settle on this: there are a lot of people that are longtime homeless.

We started to get calls from this housing program looking for aid for some of their clients that were already in permanent housing but were about to lose their housing if their financial issue wasn't resolved. Oftentimes these are one-time situations such as the loss of a job, loss of daycare (then loss of a job), car repair, death in the family, or a medical situation. All of these take the little bit of financial margin these folks have to satisfy the most urgent situation, and then the funds aren't there to pay the rent.

So after friends and family are tapped, the client reaches out to the housing program contact. In some cases the housing program is still able to provide assistance or at least partial assistance. In some cases, because of their program guidelines, the housing program is unable to step in to help financially. That's where Threshold to New Life comes in.

We are literally deemed by one of the housing program personnel as their "last resort." Now, the housing personnel contact us after they've assessed the situation. Once we've connected, they refer the client to us. We talk with the client, in person whenever possible, to see how we might help and engage them in their part of how they'll participate in the "getting back on track" effort. Often our clients do have some means to contribute so we'll look for them to do that, without tapping their last funds. It's important to have a little reserve; otherwise it will be back to the same situation.

Our clients grant us permission to discuss and negotiate with their landlord. I know we've only been at this a few years, but we rarely have a landlord who won't work with us on extending time and the payments. And in 2015, Threshold to New Life provided assistance to fifty-four people and families to help them remain in the housing they already have. And only one person, to our knowledge, lost his housing. We're still working with him as of this writing. We continue to be available to him to see him through to his dream of permanent housing.

Now, we're working with more housing programs, each with their own twist. One program we're just beginning actually needs more help up front with funds for housing applications or to open a bank account so there's a place for the disability check to be deposited. You have to have a bank account to receive your disability check, and how do you get one if you don't have ten dollars?

We started off providing relief for those in need and now are working on a model to help some of the same people become housed and live independently. The average cost we've experienced to keep someone in their housing? It's somewhere between $200 and $400. I wonder what it costs to house someone in a shelter for a month.

Oh, one last thing. You might wonder who pays for all this. Remember the *Radical* book? One of the calls to action is to live on less and give more. This can look quite different when lived out by different people. For us, it's been not replacing cars as often as we have in the past. It means when a financial obligation drops off (like a loan, mortgage, etc.) we commit to saving some of it and giving the rest away. We give first, then save and live on the rest. When I get my paycheck, by the time I check my bank balances the giving and saving money is already pulled out. We give and save first.

Why would we do this? Jesus wants our all. He demands our best. I get upset when I sort through clothing that people donate to us and the zippers don't work, items are dirty, and buttons are missing. Is that really giving or just getting rid of your junk? God wants our best and first, not our leftovers. He deserves our best. After all, he created you and has looked out for you all of your life. When you begin to believe that none of what you have is yours and you can't take it with you, you begin to value life differently than by the stuff you've accumulated. And you'll begin to experience the peace of mind that surpasses all understanding.

I didn't say it was always easy. But you have to start somewhere. So we did. Back to the question: Who pays for all this? Well, we're not the only ones that are faithfully following Jesus. There's a base of us who have chosen to give more and live on less. So, yup, that's how we're funded.

Are you up to the challenge?

About the Author

Richard Bahr is a business owner and also operates a ministry with his wife, Carla, called Threshold to New Life (www.threshold2newlife.org), helping those who live with little margin to keep the housing they have. Richard is deeply involved in serving the homeless and poor in Minneapolis by serving meals and providing clothing and other necessities, but most importantly his friendship. Proceeds from this book will work to fund the ministry.

Learn more about Threshold to New Life and follow Richard through his website at www.richardbahr.com.